Arctic Dance

My relationship with Olaus

was such an overpowering

and such a marvelous thing that

I couldn't imagine doing it or

having it or talking about it

any other way than came

to me at the time.

THE MARDY MURIE STORY

Arctic Dance

CHARLES CRAIGHEAD & BONNIE KREPS

GRAPHIC ARTS CENTER PUBLISHING®

The authors would like to thank Mardy Murie and all the members of the Murie family for allowing us to make this book, especially Louise "Weezy" Murie for patiently reading, correcting, and verifying; Steve Chase and the U.S. Fish and Wildlife Service at the National Conservation Training Center for finding the means to preserve Mardy's photographs and papers, and photographer David Swift for sensing the spirit of the project; all of Mardy's friends who contributed their time, photographs, and stories, and the many people who interviewed the Muries over the years; the various archives and museums, listed in the photo credits below, who enthusiastically helped us locate the pictures we needed; and the Craighead Environmental Research Institute for the use of material gathered during the production of *Arctic Dance: The Mardy Murie Story.*

This book is dedicated to
the intangible spirit of wild country
that inspired Mardy and Olaus.

Text © MMII by Charles Craighead and Bonnie Kreps

Book compilation © MMII by Graphic Arts Center Publishing®
An imprint of Graphic Arts Center Publishing Company
P.O. Box 10306, Portland, Oregon 97296-0306
503/226-2402   www.gacpc.com

Second printing 2006

Library of Congress Cataloging-in-Publication Data:
Craighead, Charles.
    Arctic dance : the Mardy Murie story / by Charles Craighead and
Bonnie Kreps.
        p. cm.
    ISBN 1-55868-600-2 (hardbound) — ISBN 1-55868-686-X (softbound)
    1. Murie, Margaret E. 2. Women conservationists—Alaska—Biography.
3. Environmentalists—Alaska—Biography. 4. Women pioneers—
Alaska—Biography. I. Kreps, Bonnie. II. Title.

QH31.M926 C725 2002
333.95'16'092-dc21

                                        2001007052

PRESIDENT: Charles M. Hopkins
ASSOCIATE PUBLISHER: Douglas A. Pfeiffer
EDITORIAL STAFF: Timothy W. Frew, Ellen Harkins Wheat, Tricia Brown, Jean Andrews,
    Kathy Matthews, Jean Bond-Slaughter
PRODUCTION STAFF: Richard L. Owsiany, Joanna M. Goebel
DESIGN: Elizabeth Watson

PHOTOGRAPHS: *Front cover:* Aurora, © Tom Walker; *cover inset:* Mardy in her fur trousseau, 1924, © The Murie Collection; *back cover* (clockwise from upper right): © The Murie Collection; © Thomas D. Mangelsen; © The Murie Collection; © The Murie Collection; p. 5: View from Mardy's front porch, Murie Ranch, Moose, Wyoming, 1950s; p. 6: Mardy revisits Alaska, 1978; p. 118: Olaus and Mardy hiking in Alaska.

Most photographs used in the book are courtesy of the Murie Family Collection. Many were made by Olaus Murie in the field, but some were taken by unknown photographers and copies were given to Mardy years ago without credit information. We apologize for not being able to thank those friends. Known photographers and exceptions to the Murie Collection are: p. 5, Bonnie Kreps; p. 15, Museum of History and Industry, Seattle; p. 17, Library of Congress; p. 18, Alaska State Library, Early Print of AK, PCA 01-570; p. 19, top, Yukon Archives, MacBride Museum Collection; p. 19, bottom, Library of Congress; p. 20, Library of Congress; p. 21, Library of Congress; p. 23, top, University of Alaska Fairbanks, Alaska and Polar Regions Archives, Rasmuson Library, Albert Johnson #89-166-383N; p. 23, bottom, University of Alaska Fairbanks, Alaska and Polar Regions Archives, Rasmuson Library, VF Fairbanks Break-up #76-121-14; p. 26, University of Alaska Fairbanks, Alaska and Polar Regions Archives, Rasmuson Library, Albert Johnson Box 5 #89-166-107N; p. 47, University of Alaska Fairbanks, Alaska and Polar Regions Archives, Rasmuson Library, Rufus Rose Collection #73-125-204N; p. 56, Murie Collection/Jess Rust; p. 59, Murie Collection/Jess Rust; p. 60, Murie Collection/Jess Rust; p. 69, Murie Collection/Victor B. Scheffer; p. 70, Murie Collection/Jess Rust; p. 74, Murie Collection/Mildred Capron; p. 78, Murie Collection/Mildred Capron; p. 79, top, Murie Collection/Chas G. Woodbury; p. 81, bottom, Murie Collection/Charles Ott; p. 81, right, Murie Collection/ David Swift; p. 82, Murie Collection/Edith English; p. 83, top and bottom, Murie Collection/Jim Gilligan; p. 84, top and bottom, Murie Collection/George Schaller; p.84, Murie Collection/Bob Krear; p. 86, left and right, Murie Collection/William O. Douglas; p. 87, George Schaller Collection; p. 88, Murie Collection/George Schaller; p. 91, Murie Collection/Homer W. Jewell; p. 93, Thomas D. Mangelsen; p. 95, left and right, Lyndon Baines Johnson Library; p. 96, Murie Collection/David Swift; p. 99, left, Murie Collection/David Swift; p. 102, Celia Hunter Collection; p. 105, top, Murie Collection/Barbara Barker, Moose, Wyoming; p. 105, bottom, Murie Collection/David Swift; p. 106, Jimmy Carter Library; p. 107, W. Garth Dowling, Jackson Hole, Wyoming; p. 108, Chuck Manners, Kelly, Wyoming; p. 110, Charles Craighead; p. 111, Murie Collection/David Swift; pp. 112, 113, Charles Craighead; p. 114, The White House; p. 115, Murie Collection/David Swift; p. 116, Shawn Raecke, Jackson Hole Guide.

CONTENTS

That Girl from Alaska

Two in the Far North

A Voice for the Wilderness

That Girl from Alaska

GROWING UP IN THE GREAT LAND

August 18, 1902–June 13, 1924

∼

In the air of anticipation that surrounded the turn of the century in 1900, four seemingly unrelated events occurred that helped shape the future of American conservation. Over the years they would intertwine, creating the story of one ordinary woman who accomplished extraordinary things. First, the Alaska gold rush was on, opening the

Mardy

MARDY AT AGE FOUR MONTHS,
SEATTLE, WASHINGTON, 1902

I was named for great aunt Margaret Elizabeth Thomas, and she was reputed to have raised eight children without ever raising her voice.

Mother

MARDY'S MOTHER, MINNIE EVA
FRASER, AT AGE EIGHTEEN, 1895

door to exploitation of that vast new wilderness. Second, President Theodore Roosevelt initiated his eight-year effort to establish the conservation of public land as a priority of the federal government. Third, the Wright brothers launched their first airplane, providing a means to access remote places like Alaska's bush country and giving a new perspective for appreciating the size and wonder of that land.

Grandfather Henry

MARDY WITH GRANDFATHER
HENRY FRASER IN JUNEAU, 1906

Dog cart

MARDY WITH HALF BROTHER,
FRANKLIN, AND DOG
JULIUS CAESAR

*The first memory of my life,
in Juneau, that gold-mining,
fishing town hung on a
mountainside with its feet in
Gastineau Channel, is of sitting
in a little dog cart, under an
umbrella, the cart pulled by
a black spaniel named Julius
Caesar, with my older half-
brother Franklin holding to
the back of the cart, and I,
terrified, as we whirled down
that steep street into the town.*

And then, on August 18, 1902, Margaret "Mardy" Elizabeth
Thomas came into this promising new century as a bright bud on
an unconventional and ever-changing family tree. Mardy was born
in Seattle, Washington, but her parents, Ashton Wayman Thomas
and Minnie Eva Fraser, along with Ashton's son Franklin, soon
moved north to Juneau, Alaska.

They lived in this territorial capital for the next five years.
Ashton Thomas was an enterprising businessman, and Juneau was
the first boomtown of the Alaska gold rush. Mardy was too young
to be aware of the town's atmosphere of promise, but she never
forgot its steep terrain. Ashton had come west from Grand Manan
Island, New Brunswick, in 1883, to escape the endless hard work he

Mardy

MARDY AT AGE FOUR-AND-A-HALF
YEARS, JUNEAU, 1906

Aunt Bertha

MARDY WITH AUNT BERTHA
FRASER, JUNEAU

Mardy, 1907

MARDY AT AGE FIVE YEARS,
SEATTLE, 1907

saw as his future there. Minnie had also been born and raised on Grand Manan, and had left the island herself in order to see more of the world. It seems to have been their common heritage that first brought Ashton and Minnie together. But in 1907 Ashton and Minnie divorced, and Minnie returned to Seattle with five-year-old Mardy. With news of the divorce, Minnie's mother moved west from the family home on Grand Manan Island to take care of Mardy so Minnie could enroll in business school and support herself.

In 1910 Minnie Thomas fell in love and remarried, to a Seattle attorney named Louis R. Gillette. He worked in the federal court system and had spent time in Alaska, and in 1911 he was assigned to be Assistant U.S. Attorney in the Fairbanks office. Congress had recently given the northern territory its own civil and criminal codes, and Louis Gillette was sent to Fairbanks to help bring law and order to the frontier. Once he arrived and found housing, he

Steamship to Skagway

MARDY AND HER MOTHER SAILED FROM SEATTLE TO SKAGWAY, ALASKA, ON THE STEAMSHIP *JEFFERSON*, 1911.

Mardy, 1910

MARDY AT AGE EIGHT
WITH HER MOTHER
AND STEPFATHER,
LOUIS R. GILLETTE

sent a telegram to his wife and daughter, asking them to catch the last steamship north before winter's ice closed down transportation on the Alaskan rivers.

Just at a time when twentieth-century technology was starting to make its impact on the country, Mardy left civilization behind to go live where there was no running water and the mail arrived by sleigh and dogsled. The only commercial route from Seattle to

Frontier luxury

MARDY AND HER MOTHER STAYED IN SKAGWAY'S PULLEN HOUSE, IN 1911, FAMOUS THROUGHOUT THE NORTH FOR ITS ELEGANCE.

Dawson City

DAWSON STREET SCENE, CA. 1898

their home in Fairbanks was a three-week trip by steamship, train, riverboat, and finally horse-drawn cart. For a nine-year-old girl, it was a time to watch the landscape unfold, to adjust to new ways of daily living, and to take her own measure of the frontier. Mardy's vivid childhood memories of this epic journey seemed to set the stage for her somewhat nomadic lifestyle; long before Alaska became a state, she would travel up and down the length of

Sternwheeler from Dawson to Tanana

▲ *She [sternwheeler Sarah] was, it seemed to me, enormous, both long and broad, and with a great space up front on the main deck, under the upper deck, and inside, a large "saloon" all done up in green plush and white paneling and gold trimming, like a drawingroom in a fairy-tale palace. Besides this there was a card room, where the men gathered, and a ladies' lounge where the women sat with their needlework and their talk.*

Sternwheeler pilot

◄ *The Sarah was even more exciting than the Jefferson. From all the adult conversation I listened to, I gathered that we were lucky to catch her on this last trip, that she was the queen of the fleet, that her captain "knew the river," and she "had the best food."*

Chena River

CHENA RIVER AND BUILDINGS
IN FAIRBANKS

Growing up in Fairbanks, one knew no other town. There were no others nearer than eight days by horse sleigh or ten days by river steamer. So we children of Fairbanks were early accustomed to all kinds of people—they were taken for granted, part of the environment we knew. Not until I was nearly grown and at last went Outside to school did I begin to realize that our town was indeed different.

Alaska's southeast coast seven times and journey thousands of miles crisscrossing the Territory.

Fairbanks in 1911 was a booming gold rush town. It had a population of about 5,000—with twenty-three saloons and five churches. It was not only life on the edge of the wilderness, but on the edge of the rules of society. Its inhabitants had been lured to this harsh but promising place from all over the world, and they created a new social structure to reflect their diverse backgrounds.

The colorful and down-to-earth life in Fairbanks had a great influence on young Mardy Thomas—she kept her father's name— and it taught her a friendly and accepting way of living that would become a big part of her character. In contrast to the Victorian world of Seattle and the Lower 48 states, Fairbanks was a place of many tastes and standards. There was also no room to hide— everyone knew everybody's business. But in the course of daily life in the Arctic it was a person's basic character that mattered most. Mardy learned early on to see the goodness in hard-living prospectors and trappers, and not to judge them by their rough appearance.

In Fairbanks, Mardy learned the importance of self-discipline in keeping up with day-to-day chores—preparing food supplies for winter, chopping wood, and building fires. She also learned the Fairbanks custom of holding regular social events to help ward off feelings of isolation and loneliness. Mardy learned to set

Alaskan summer

▶ FAIRBANKS HOUSE, GARDENS, CATS

So went the glorious summer, short in days but almost of double length thanks to the heavenly, stimulating twenty-four hour daylight. The days were often so warm that people were content to sit with sewing or a book on the porches in the afternoons.

Mardy's dog, Major

Nearly all the children in Fairbanks at a certain age had a dog, and the dogs were practically all Siberian huskies. And on the weekends we kids were all over town, with our dogs hitched to little coaster sleds, running errands for our mothers and doing all kinds of little treks here and there. And sometimes also getting our dogs into fights. And these gentlemen from the creeks—that was the term used for the gold-mining area around Fairbanks: "He's out in the creeks"—well, in the wintertime they just sort of watched what was going on all over town, and they took care of us.

everything aside and relax for a few moments each day, no matter what the hardships were. The small comforts of a four o'clock tea, home-baked cookies, and warm conversation became central to her well-being and way of life.

The contrasting lifestyles of the white-collar families of Fairbanks and the itinerant, rowdy miners no doubt helped give Mardy a better sense of her own place in the world. At all levels of society she saw fortunes squandered, marriages come and go, new careers take shape, and people's lives change dramatically with one event. She saw that through it all, things seemed to work out, and people usually found a way to get along. She also learned the strength of her family, living in a home where everyone pitched in.

Hauling wood

▸▲ EVERY FAIRBANKS FAMILY USED AT LEAST NINE CORDS PER WINTER.

Chena River breakup

▸ *The fire siren would sound and the "six o'clock whistle" in quick short blasts. The ice was going!*

Winter

TAKING CARE OF SISTER LOUISE

*Walking into the sunrise on
the way to school, half a mile,
smoke going straight up in the
perfectly still air, which meant
20 below or more. Some days it
will be 50 or 60 below and
sometimes it will be 50 below
for weeks. But life goes on.
Businessmen in coonskin
overcoats and caps hurry to
open their stores and build up
fires in the big stoves.*

THAT GIRL FROM ALASKA

Mardy had her own daily household chores with her mother, and she helped care for her half sister, Louise, and half brother, Louis.

The winter she was fourteen, her father, Ashton Thomas, came back into her life. Mardy hadn't seen him for as long as she could remember, but he and Minnie had kept in touch, and he wrote to ask permission for Mardy to visit him. He now owned a salmon cannery in Prince William Sound and invited Mardy to come visit him the following summer in Port Ashton. He had remarried, and both his new wife and Mardy's half brother, Franklin, would be there.

Mardy was nervous about the family politics of making the trip to be reacquainted with her father, but as she packed her bags she heard her mother's calm and forgiving voice saying, "Don't worry, meeting your father will be like a big warm breeze carrying you away."

The journey south in the spring of 1918 was a remarkable adventure for fifteen-year-old Mardy, for it marked both the end of

Home

MARDY BY LOG HOME, 1914

Daddy found one vacant house—one way out on the edge of town, eight blocks from the river, the last house on the last street of the Fairbanks of that year. It was log, of course, and sturdy, but with only four rooms. This cabin was home for ten years.

Valdez Trail

VALDEZ TRAIL ROADHOUSE
AND SLEIGH

Delicious food—moose steak—and sweet sleep. We left in the dusky dark again, at midnight. There was a couple of hours when I lay curled up in the wolfskin robe on the seat, half asleep while the sled whispered along fairly smoothly, a sleepy sound, broken only once in a while by a quiet voice: "Ish—get in there, Brownie." It seemed like we had been traveling like this for weeks.

the horse-drawn era and the beginning of her own independence—she would travel without her parents on the very last commercial sleigh to negotiate the 375-mile Valdez Trail. The first leg of the trip entailed a week of traveling through the Alaska Range by horse-drawn sleigh, over melting spring snow and treacherous stream crossings. This late in the year much of the traveling was done at night, when the snow and ice set up enough to support the sleigh. Late each night they stopped in one of the colorful roadhouses sprinkled along the way—Salcha, Sullivan's, Rapids, Meier's, or Big Delta.

Once they had crossed the mountains and dropped down to a snow-free lower elevation near the coast, Mardy transferred to a wheeled wagon for two days of plodding along muddy trails to reach the little town of Chitina. From there she took a train to Cordova, on the Gulf of Alaska, and boarded a ship headed for Evans Island, in Prince William Sound.

Port Ashton, located on a large bay on Evans Island, was named for Mardy's father. He had built an extensive salmon and herring cannery, and had named his business—the Franklin Packing Company—after Mardy's half brother. When Mardy

George Markham was the next driver. He was older, serious, educated, of solid opinions. He took wonderful care of me and discoursed on life and love and marriage in Alaska. Near the Copper River, the country ahead, green hills rising to snowy mountains, looked inviting and different. "Well," said George as we slogged along, "We'll be in Copper Center tonight, a real nice place. So your big journey is about over—nine days of—whoa there!" The old horse was only too willing to stop. George stooped to the ground by the horse's left hind foot. There in the clod of mud raised by the hoof shone two silver dollars. He wiped the coins off on his trousers and handed me one. "Keep this always. It's your lucky dollar." I still have that dollar. I wonder if George Markham kept his?

Father

MARDY'S FATHER, ASHTON THOMAS

Why did Father go West? It was nothing but hard work back there on Grand Manan—no adventure, no time for anything but work. So he left, he and Uncle John and Turner Watt. They came by train to Frisco, and up the coast by boat, and they got to Port Townsend in 1883. That was a busy port then, but among all the ships, there were the Indians, out there in their canoes and other little boats, pulling in king salmon hand over fist as fast as they could, and Father looked at that and he said, "Boys, this is far enough!"

So they came to Seattle and worked on boats, and later to the San Juan Islands. Father was sheriff of San Juan County in 1896, and married Katie Thornton.

Father and some others had built this new boat, the Katie Thornton, *at Friday Harbor, and they sailed her to Anacortes to register her. And while they were tied up there a ship came in and on board were some men from California looking for a place to start a salmon cannery, and the captain told them, "The man you ought to talk to is Ashton Thomas." So Father talked to these men—one was named Devlin—and it turned out that he stayed with them on their boat and left Uncle John to take the* Katie Thornton *back, and that was the beginning of the first cannery at Friday Harbor.*

—Franklin Thomas, to his half sister, Mardy

Picnic

FRANKLIN PACKING COMPANY
ANNUAL PICNIC. MARDY AND HER
FATHER IN BACK ROW.

arrived she was greeted warmly by the members of her extended family—father, stepmother, uncles and cousins, and half brother— and she was immediately plunged into the hectic and olfactory world of an Alaska fisheries business.

Her stepmother was experienced in living outdoors, and she introduced young Mardy to the joys of exploring the countless bays and inlets of Prince William Sound. They would go off for four or five days at a time in a little clinker-built boat with a small outboard engine. Mardy later wrote of the experience: "That first summer gave me a picture of that part of Alaska, a knowledge of camping skills, and a respect for tide and storm. We went through all the islands and their enticing coves. We hiked to the upper reaches of many of the islands. We watched a fight between a large whale and a killer whale. We explored, we had our adventures, we came back safely and told Father where we had been, and he nearly always said, "Good Lord, what were you doing way out there?"

I was suddenly plunged into the warm and vigorous and lively life of a family seagoing fisheries business, totally alien to all I had known. I couldn't tie a bowline, I couldn't steer a seine boat, I couldn't read the compass. Worst of all, I couldn't row.

But I learned to row, out among the beautiful bays and inlets, with the whales and the puffins.

Family piano

MUSIC AND DANCING
WERE THE CENTER
OF SOCIAL LIFE
IN FRONTIER ALASKA.

Dressed up

MARDY, SUMMER 1922

At the end of that invigorating summer, Mardy returned to the routine of school. In Fairbanks, she had many bright and dedicated teachers. The three Rs were strictly taught, and she was encouraged to spend much of her spare time reading and writing. Both her stepfather and her own father were avid readers and enjoyed learning about the world, and they instilled that passion in her. She was taught that her own curiosity was a gift. Her stepfather once said to her, "Curiosity, that divine thing, curiosity. It will carry you on when all else fails." Mardy took that advice to heart, and it carried her through many trials and hardships later in life.

Then came the trips out to college and back, and three summers spent at my father's fish cannery in Prince William Sound. In all of this, the steamers were the only transportation in those days. They were the queens of that Southeast world; and those eight or more trips, Seattle to Skagway and back again, live on with me as a glowing chapter of my life.

I was on my way home to Fairbanks when I heard that someone up there had an airplane. Little did I realize at that moment how life in Alaska would be changed by this news.

Simmons College, 1922

My junior year of college was spent at Simmons in Boston, where I got to be known as "that girl from Alaska."

After completing high school in 1919, Mardy decided to go on to Reed College, in Portland, Oregon. She had met a woman professor from Reed, Bertha K. Young, and had been inspired by Bertha's enthusiasm to continue her formal education. So, in late summer she left Fairbanks again, this time as a paying passenger in a Model T Ford. Their route followed the same old rutted wagon and sleigh trails, which were slowly being converted to automobile use. After three rough days by car to the coast, she sailed west to visit her relatives in Port Ashton, and then caught the steamship to Seattle. From there she took a train to Portland.

This was obviously an unusual extended family in which Mardy was growing up. Neither her mother's nor her father's side seemed to think anything of jaunting off to some remote port, of uprooting and starting life over, or of sending young Mardy off alone into the world. There may have been a safer and more trusting atmosphere at that time and in that part of the world, but the Thomases and Gillettes seemed to excel in moving freely about. They were also unusually supportive of the independence

Olaus

Olaus Murie was an arctic biologist who spent most of his time in the wild. He had come to Alaska in 1920 after spending three years in the Canadian Arctic. He could travel and work in the desolate northern winters, and he spoke the Native Eskimo language. Olaus was also a talented artist, and like other great turn-of-the-century naturalists he illustrated his field notes with his own detailed paintings.
—from the
film narration,
Arctic Dance

and education of women in the family, with Mardy and her adventurous stepmother as prime examples. Although Mardy credits frontier Alaska with shaping her spirit, this unconventional family life probably had as much to do with her carefree nature as anything.

When Mardy joined the five hundred other students at Reed College she discovered an almost painful shyness in herself, and although she made friends with some of the girls, she avoided social events and had few men friends. But her schooling was excellent and progressive, and Mardy was inspired by her teachers to fulfill her own sense of adventure. She attended Reed for two years, traveling north in the summer to work for her father as the cannery storekeeper in Port Ashton.

In the summer of 1921, Ashton Thomas told Mardy he had arranged to spend the next winter in Boston, Massachusetts, on business, and Mardy made the decision to join him there. She transferred her school records to Simmons College, in Boston, and then returned to Fairbanks for two months before going east.

After the impersonal atmosphere of college, Mardy relished the warmth of her family and friends in Fairbanks. It was while visiting her old friend and neighbor Jess Rust that she learned of a new man in town, a handsome young biologist named Olaus Murie.

Mardy wasn't immediately impressed with Olaus, but over the next few weeks they spent time together, mainly through the efforts of Jess Rust to include both of them in social events. Olaus's intelligence and talent began to show through his quiet manner, and by the time Mardy went east to continue her English studies in Boston, they had agreed to stay in touch. Olaus then left by dogsled for the Brooks Range to study caribou for the winter.

Neither one of them knew it yet, but Olaus's early life had a curious similarity to Mardy's. He was born in 1889, thirteen years before Mardy, in a frame house on the windswept prairie near Moorhead, Minnesota. His parents were Norwegian immigrants, Joachim and Marie Murie, who had come to the United States just a year before Olaus was born.

Joachim Murie died when Olaus was seven years old and his brother, Martin, was four. After a time Marie Murie married a Swede named Ed Wickstrom and they named their first child Adolph. But Ed Wickstrom died just two years later, leaving

Olaus

OLAUS ON BOAT DECK IN HUDSON BAY, 1915

Jess Rust had come home from work one night and said, "Today I met the man that Mardy ought to marry." I was just there for vacation, between two years at Reed College and then off to Simmons, but in the meantime, Jess invited Olaus for dinner, and they brought me over there. And I was in the kitchen helping Clara with the baby when they came in, so when I was introduced to the slim, blue-eyed Norwegian, I had my hands full of baby bottles . . . And then at dinner Clara said, "Well, your name is Scottish, isn't it?" and he said, "No, Norwegian," and I thought "Ah-ha." Ever since I was four years old I had told my mother (she had told me this later on) that when I grew up I was going to marry a Norwegian.

Somehow I still did not know this quiet young scientist, always sweet and pleasant and agreeable. Something was missing. One evening the gang were all at our dining table making Christmas cards, Olaus helping us with the drawings. Over some question of mine and his usual sweet answer, I suddenly snapped: "Oh, what everlasting good nature!"

He turned to me, and the blue eyes were steely: "Look, if you want a fight, you can have it!"

Here was more than a pleasant companion. Here was a man—gentle, but with steel within.

Olaus's birthplace

The Murie home in Kragnes, Minnesota, where Olaus was born on March 1, 1889

Marie with all three boys to raise. She took the Murie name again and went to work doing laundry and cleaning the nearby church, and the boys helped out by delivering milk and firewood. Olaus was the oldest and took his younger brothers under his wing. They were all bright boys. They read and studied diligently, and Olaus's gift for drawing was encouraged.

After high school Olaus won a scholarship to Fargo College, across the river in North Dakota. He then transferred to Pacific University in Forest Grove, Oregon. He graduated in 1912 as a biologist, and immediately went north into the Canadian Arctic on assignment for the Carnegie Museum. He served in the Army Balloon Corps in World War I, then joined the U.S. Biological Survey, which was the predecessor to the U.S. Fish and Wildlife Service. His first assignment was to assist the eminent, but notoriously grouchy, biologist E. W. Nelson study the life history of the caribou of Alaska.

In 1922, not long after he first met Mardy in Fairbanks, Olaus learned that his brother Martin had died of tuberculosis back in Minnesota. Martin, also a biologist, had planned to join Olaus in Alaska to assist on the caribou study, so when Olaus was in Minnesota he invited his younger half brother, Adolph, to take Martin's place as his assistant. They were engaged in this study while Olaus and Mardy were becoming acquainted.

Norwegian immigrants

OLAUS'S PARENTS,
JOACHIM AND MARIE
MURIE, ON THEIR
WEDDING DAY

In July 1920, Dr. E. W. Nelson, chief of the U.S. Biological Survey, was accompanying a new young biologist named Olaus Murie to begin studies of the Alaska-Yukon caribou. They traveled by steamer to Nome, and then up the Yukon and the Tanana to Fairbanks. At every stop the steamer made, Olaus was off, away from the settlement, collecting specimens. Dr. Nelson gave him a scolding, saying that he thought Olaus should be meeting the people of the villages and towns, getting acquainted; this might be useful to him in his work later on. Olaus's reaction was: "Just leave me alone up here for six months, and then if you are not satisfied you can fire me."

In Boston, Mardy moved in with her father's family. With his encouragement, she took courses in business administration at Simmons, as well as in her major of English. By late winter, Ashton Thomas had become ill and returned to Seattle with his family. (He would die there just four years later.) So Mardy was on her own in Boston, and moved into a Simmons' dormitory with sixteen other girls. She was different from the rest of the young women there, and was known on campus as "that girl from Alaska." Without her father's and stepmother's company, Mardy left Simmons after that spring semester of her junior year, and she returned to Fairbanks to decide how, and where, to continue her education.

Meanwhile she went to work as clerk to the U.S. Attorney, living at home to help care for her small stepbrother and stepsister and singing in the church choir with her stepfather. Her mother was working as a secretary for the Bureau of Mines at this time. Mardy also joined in the active social life of the younger Fairbanks women and men, going out to dances, picnics, and on hikes. Since dancing was a big part of life in Fairbanks, Mardy and her friends spent many evenings with the Victrola, learning all the latest steps and enjoying the musical hits of the period. Each week a big community dance was held, and everyone went.

Dog booties

DOG TEAMS WERE ESSENTIAL TO ARCTIC LIFE, AND THEY WERE WELL CARED FOR.

Arctic expedition, 1922

◀ ADOLPH AND ▾ OLAUS—THE
STRENUOUS LIFE OF A BIOLOGIST

*The next year Dr. Nelson
suggested that Olaus's brother
Adolph might go up from
Minnesota (he was a junior
in college) and be Olaus's
assistant, and that is when
they made the famous trip,
with two dog teams, from
Fairbanks to the Koyukuk
country, and the Kobuk,
and back via the Chandalar
and the Yukon and to Circle
and so back to Fairbanks.*

Picnic

MARDY, OLAUS, AND

FRIENDS ON A PICNIC

Olaus was working in the backcountry most of that summer of 1922, but in preparation for his winter-long dogsled trip with Adolph, he was in town for two months. The people of Fairbanks made the most of their brief, nightless summer, holding a round-the-clock schedule of parties, picnics, and dances. Olaus joined in the fun, but he had spent most of his time with his studies or in the field and had never learned to dance. Mardy wouldn't have anything to do with a man who couldn't dance, so she taught him to a tune fittingly called "The Hesitation Waltz."

The winter of 1922–23 found Mardy busily working and attending social events. Many eligible young men called on her, but she had started a beautiful and unusual correspondence with Olaus Murie while he was out in the wilderness. Mardy's frequent letters would go off by dogsled to a village somewhere ahead of Olaus, to collect and await his arrival. Olaus would reply to them as he traveled and camped, and at each opportunity he mailed off his replies. Sometimes three or four letters from Olaus would arrive at once, and Mardy read each letter in order, first in her room alone and

One day we went on a trip upriver, and at one place in the quiet water of Moose Creek we heard a great-horned owl hoot far off in the forest. Olaus answered him. Again the owl spoke, a bit closer this time. Olaus hooted again, and so it went, until suddenly out of nowhere the dark soft shape floated into a treetop right above us. That made an impression on me. What kind of magic did this man have?

A good book

MARDY READING
AT HOME WHILE
OLAUS WAS ON HIS
DOGSLED EXPEDITION
WITH ADOLPH

Olaus carried an art kit, which had been a map kit from the infantry, and he wore that on his hip. It had the porcelain slide to mix the watercolor paint, different from our ordinary watercolor paint. He had discovered early on that when collecting specimens, the color would fade within twenty minutes of the bird or whatever being killed. So he carried his paints with him and he would just sit down and do a painting.

then aloud to her family, omitting what her stepfather discreetly called the "and so forth parts."

From the Koyukuk Trail, December 23, 1922:

Mardy Dear,

By strange chance there is a possible opportunity to send out a letter—all because a man left his teeth behind! It is this way. A man started in for the Koyukuk ahead of us, as a passenger with the mailman. At a cabin where they stopped one night he put aside his false teeth and the next day went off without them! He met a trapper up here somewhere and paid him to make a dash back there and then try to catch us here, at the "80-mile cabin." The trapper came in here tonight with the teeth. We will catch the poor man at Alatna in two days, and will turn over to him his dental apparatus. But the thing that interests me is Mr. Jones, the trapper, although headed for his camp right now, is going in to Tanana about the first, probably ten days ahead of the mailman, and so will be the means of getting this to you and help me talk to you again—God bless him!

My ink isn't quite thawed yet, but there is enough to dip the pen into. This works all right for frozen ink, don't you think?

Olaus

In the summer of 1924, Olaus was in charge of an expedition to Hooper Bay with a party of six, on a waterfowl study. To reach Hooper Bay meant 700 miles of trail, with several dog teams. Meanwhile, back in Fairbanks, I was planning our wedding and getting ready to graduate from the University of Alaska.

How I wish you were with me right now. We are up on a summit, the night is silver clear, with twinkling stars and a pure crescent moon. I was out a moment ago to look at it and think of you at the same time. The spruces stand all around, straight and still. The dogs lie curled in dark blurs on the snow. The very smoke from the cabin pipe floats up so still and soft. Oh, the sweet silence of a moonlit night!

Olaus

Thus by spring Mardy and Olaus knew each other well, and their feelings for each other had deepened. In the summer of 1923, Mardy and her mother went to visit Olaus at his caribou research camp near Mount McKinley. After five days of what Mardy called "tramping about in a rosy haze in those enchanted mountains," Mardy and Olaus knew for certain they would marry.

With that, it was time for a practical decision. Olaus needed to go to Washington, D.C., for the winter to write reports on his field work, so it seemed a perfect time for Mardy to finish her college education. The Alaska Agricultural College and School of Mines (later called the University of Alaska) had just opened its doors in Fairbanks the year before, and although there was no English department for her major, it was now offering a business degree. Mardy could switch majors and graduate the following spring. She would be the only senior in a student body of fifty-two.

Olaus returned to Fairbanks for a few weeks in March to prepare for his next wilderness research trip, a five-month excursion to the Bering Sea Coast to study waterfowl. That project would be followed immediately by a three-month journey by boat and by dogsled above the Arctic Circle to the Endicott Mountains in the Brooks Range. Before Olaus left for Hooper Bay on the Bering Sea, they picked Mardy's birthday, August 18, for a tentative wedding date. Mardy's mother had enough faith in Olaus's reliability that she ordered engraved wedding invitations with that date from the printers in Seattle.

Mardy worked at finishing her schooling, with no word from Olaus for months. On June 13, 1924, she received her business degree from the Alaska Agricultural College and School of Mines and became the first woman graduate of the school. She was ready to leave home and join Olaus Murie in the wilderness.

First woman graduate

1924, University of Alaska, Fairbanks

Two in the Far North

EXPLORING THE WILDS WITH OLAUS

June 14, 1924–October 21, 1963

~

After her graduation, Mardy Thomas began immediately to prepare for her new life as the wife of an arctic biologist. Her wedding would be far from civilization, eight hundred miles down the Yukon River in the small riverside village of Anvik. Her mother tried to balance Mardy's unconventional wedding plans with traditional showers, tea parties, and

Fur trousseau

I had all these things—
the fur parka, the fur boots,
the moccasins. And my mother's
friends would stop by. . . .
"We came to see the funny
trousseau!"

1920s Alaska

MAP OF HONEYMOON
FROM MARDY'S MEMOIR
TWO IN THE FAR NORTH

MARRIAGE CERTIFICATE

OLAUS'S DRAWINGS OF
THEIR WEDDING CAKE AND
THE CHURCH IN ANVIK

Map labels:

SIBERIA

ARCTIC OCEAN

POINT BARROW

Barrow

BERING STRAIT

ST. LAWRENCE I.

Kotzebue

COLVILLE R.

BROOKS RANGE

KONGAKUT R.

Demarcation Point

Nome

Arctic Village

Wiseman

Bettles

KOBUK R.

NOATAK R.

BERING

Nulato

KOYUKUK R.

Fort Yukon

PORCUPINE R.

COLEEN R.

CANADA

NUNIVAK I.

St. Michael

Anvik

Holy Cross

YUKON R.

Fairbanks

YUKON R.

SEA

KUSKOKWIM R.

Kantishna

MT. McKINLEY

ALASKA RANGE

TANANA R.

Dawson

YUKON R.

NUSHAGAN R.

Anchorage

Valdez

ALASKA PENINSULA

KODIAK I.

GULF OF ALASKA

Skagway

Juneau

Sitka

Ketchikan

ALASKA

Miles
0   100   200   map by palacios

I suppose the most unusual thing about this wedding was the hour at which it was held. Three o'clock in the morning. I felt a great wave of gratitude when Mother and I stepped out on the deck of the General Jacobs *and found all the rest of the party waiting, perfectly groomed at that hour, and for us! Under the deck lights stood Elizabeth, my dearest friend, in cream lace and a flowery cloche; the light glinted on the captain's gold buttons; the engineer was startlingly handsome, having scrubbed away the engine room grease and sporting gray suede gloves and a fedora.*

I turned to catch a happy reassuring smile from Mother, and saw that she was wearing a big pink rose Mrs. Webster had given us from her hothouse at Tanana on our way downriver. Roses were rare, precious gems in Alaska, and yet here was one at our wedding far down the Yukon.

Wedding ship

THE STERNWHEELER *GENERAL J. W. JACOBS* CARRIED MARDY AND HER WEDDING PARTY 800 MILES DOWN THE YUKON RIVER TO MEET OLAUS.

receptions, but at the same time Mardy was busy packing her trousseau of fur parkas, mittens, snowshoes, wool knickers, and a sturdy tent and camp stove. Her honeymoon was to be a three-month trip by boat and by dog team while Olaus continued his caribou studies in the Upper Koyukuk River country.

Mardy's wish to join Olaus in the wilderness, as she had written so often in her letters to him, was about to come true. This independent young woman was now going to embark on an expedition that would take her into the very heart of the wild North. Her memories of this exhilarating trip, and her growing passion to keep the Great Land from being overrun by civilization, would eventually give her a prominent role in determining Alaska's future.

Her wedding party left Fairbanks in mid-August and headed down the Yukon River aboard the sternwheel steamer *General J. W. Jacobs*. With her were her mother and Elizabeth Romig, her best friend and bridesmaid. At the same time, Olaus started upriver in a small open boat from his field camp in Hooper Bay, bringing with

Nulato, 1924

❧

OLAUS AND MARDY
WERE DROPPED OFF IN
NULATO BY THE
GENERAL J.W. JACOBS.
THEY WAITED THERE TEN
DAYS FOR A BOAT TO TAKE
THEM UP THE KOYUKUK
RIVER TO THE VILLAGE OF
BETTLES, TO BEGIN THEIR
DOGSLED TRIP TO THE
BROOKS RANGE.

The Wedding Ship

Nulato

Apart from the World

We had the warm light of a kerosene lamp on the table, the cheerful crackling from the stove; and to make it complete, as darkness fell the rain came again, a soft patter on the tin roof, with a whisper of wind.

him the associate chief of the U.S. Biological Survey to act as best man. Mardy and Olaus hadn't seen each other for five months. The two boats met up at the village of Holy Cross on the intended day, August 18, and after a tearful reunion aboard the *General Jacobs,* the party steamed back upriver to Anvik to meet the minister and his family of missionaries. The midnight hour ending her birthday passed during the slow upstream trip, so Mardy and Olaus were married in Anvik's log chapel at three o'clock in the morning, August 19, 1924.

Mardy and Olaus said farewell to the wedding party at the village of Nulato,

Housekeeping

MARDY CUTTING FIREWOOD,
NULATO, 1924

Otto Geist

▶ OTTO AND DOG
IN NENANA, ALASKA

and the *General Jacobs* churned on to Fairbanks. The newly-weds waited ten days in Nulato for the river steamer *Teddy H* to take them up the Koyukuk River toward the village of Bettles to meet their dog team. On their journey aboard the *Teddy H* they became friends with one of the ship's engineers, a young German archaeologist named Otto Geist. He remained a close friend of the Muries for the rest of his life. Otto went on to study the Eskimos' history and establish a museum of archaeology at the university in Fairbanks.

Mardy's epic honeymoon journey in the wilderness with Olaus set the tone for their marriage and careers. Olaus went about his work, but he now had a partner who brought a civilized touch to his camps, and witnessed with him the wild beauty that had been

Olaus & Mardy

※

OLAUS AND MARDY
IN THEIR TRAIL FURS

*I remember once saying to
Olaus on our dogsled
honeymoon, "Whatever
made you think I could
do all this?" And he
looked at me and he said,
"Oh, I knew you could."*

On the trail with team, November 3, 1924

❋

When the trail was good at all, I'd stand on the handlebars; otherwise, I'd have to run. And those Alaska dogs were so eager to get into harness and go that you could hardly restrain them in the morning. They would go so fast that I just had to hang on to this curved handlebar at the back of the sled, and sometimes my arm and my feet would be flying out behind somewhere.

Our sled was made by a marvelous Norwegian gentleman in Fairbanks, and it was fifteen feet long. You put all your gear in, first a whole layer of smoked salmon for the dogs, and then all your gear and food and sleeping bags and everything on top of that, and the canvas came up over and was tied in various ways. And then the two bars from the side of the sled stuck out and there was a brake attached underneath to help stop the dogs. In rough terrain Olaus would cut from a spruce tree a long pole that he tied toward the front of the sled, and he ran there to help steer the sled and help the dogs over the rough places. That was called a gee pole, and was part of the equipment that I had to learn about.

his home the past few years. Together, they endured the hardships of arctic travel, discussed the arts while Olaus dissected caribou specimens, and discovered a shared taste for a simple but rewarding life in the wilderness. For Mardy, this man who loved to explore must have fit right in with her own family's adventurous roots. By the time they had finished the 550-mile dogsled trip and returned to Fairbanks, they both knew they had found a perfect world.

The married life

Alone in an eight-by-ten tent with three caribou hides . . . no reading matter. I was learning a bit more about being married to a scientist.

53

Journal entry

MUSHING IN KOYUKUK COUNTRY

The usual dog team was seven dogs—three pairs and a leader. Ours were Siberian huskies, with prick ears and a curly tail, and beautiful black and gray and white markings, and crazy to run. The average day would be about 20, 24 miles, something like that, but if it was a tough trail, if you made 19 miles you felt thankful.

There was one roadhouse up there in that whole Koyukuk country, and we got there about six o'clock and the roadhouse man heard us coming and came rushing out with an old-fashioned lantern. He said, "An Indian came by today and said you were coming the overland trail. And that's no place for a woman." It was a tough trail, but that's the way we had to go.

We leave the smokes of Bettles behind us + strike north — Oct. 19

Fishing

I think I actually landed five grayling, but one was a large one and I was very proud of it, so Olaus took a picture of me with this big grayling hanging down from my hand. That was part of that happy month at Bettles, just waiting for freeze-up, going on little trips every day, running a little trap line for mice and whatever little creatures—Olaus was always learning and studying and gathering data about everything.

They spent the rest of that first winter together in Washington, D.C., near the Biological Survey headquarters while Olaus wrote his report on the Hooper Bay expedition. Then, in the spring, he was sent to a remote portion of the Alaska Peninsula to study brown bears. Mardy was pregnant with their first child, and she went to Twisp, Washington, where her mother and stepfather had moved from Fairbanks to set up a private law practice and to escape the harsh Alaska winters. That summer, Mardy gave birth to their son, Martin, on July 10, 1925. Olaus was unable to leave Alaska for another month, but received a telegram telling him the good news.

Baby Martin, 1925

MARDY WITH BABY MARTIN—
THE "MILLION DOLLAR YAWN"

*Olaus had been out on the
Alaska Peninsula on a brown
bear study for six months and
did not see his son until the
baby was three months old.*

In the fall, the Muries returned to Washington, D.C., while
Olaus wrote another report, this one documenting his years
of caribou study. They stayed until April, when Olaus was assigned
to explore the remote headwaters of the Old Crow River in northeastern Alaska. Mardy knew this was a critical time in her life with
Olaus; she had spent the winter on the East Coast with what she
called "the Biological Survey wives" and knew she was expected to

Poling upriver

OLAUS AND MARDY POLING THEIR SCOW UP THE OLD CROW,
WITH YOUNG MARTIN IN A TENT ON DECK

Somebody had told the head of the Biological Survey that the Old Crow River country was a wonderful waterfowl place and that some scientist should be sent up there. So Olaus was sent, and our friend Jesse Rust got leave from his job to go along. I wasn't going to be left behind, so the baby and I came, too. And then about the third day up the river the crankshaft broke. Olaus said to Jess, "I'm willing to pole while you tug the tow line, if you're willing." And so we had about 250 more miles to go that way.

The Old Crow River is just a sluggish, muddy stream that meanders across a Pleistocene lake bed. I think the thing that saved our friendship and our sanity was the singing. Jess remembered a lot of old-time songs and had a nice tenor voice. I had been brought up singing. We sang our way up 250 miles of that river.

Old Crow

MARDY WITH BABY MARTIN—
IN OLD CROW VILLAGE

We said our good-byes at three-thirty, with everybody gathered on the bank again. A young woman and a little four-year-old girl came up to me. The child handed Martin a package, a pair of moccasins, made since our arrival. The young woman spoke some English. "My little girl, she crazy about baby. She cry. She say, "Oh, Mama, make some moccasins quick. . . . "

stay home and raise their baby. But her heart told her to travel into the wilderness. So she packed up the baby and joined Olaus in Fairbanks for the planned journey up the Old Crow River. They were joined on this trip by their old friend and neighbor from Fairbanks, Jess Rust.

The Muries' arctic dogsled trip two winters earlier had been a lark compared to the Old Crow expedition. Isolation, hard labor, fickle weather, cold rain, mud, equipment breakdowns, and ultimately a lack of scientific accomplishments made this trip more than memorable. Worst of all, they discovered that in summer even the local Indians abandoned that part of the Arctic because of the horrendous mosquitoes. But Mardy accepted the bad with the good, and continued to see the beauty of this untouched land. Even when their motorboat died and they had to pole it by hand another 250 miles, her diary reflected her joy of discovery and the peace to be experienced when traveling through an uninhabited world:

The river was empty, the other shore just a thick green wall. At my back, behind the little tent, stretched the limitless tundra,

Martin

MARTIN IN HIS CRIB

I used empty five-gallon gasoline cans for the dishes and for clothes, where the cans would be cut down through the center and the sides rolled back to make a handle. You can put it on the fire and warm some water for the diapers. And the diapers you just hang over the willow bushes. And in the other tin you prepared food and did all of the next day's preparations. I had a double boiler for the baby's mush that I fed him in the morning.

Jess & Olaus

"Two Bums of the Old Crow"

There's one picture from the Old Crow trip where Olaus and Jess both let their beards grow. But Olaus never could stand it for very long.

Tea break

JESS, MARDY, AND OLAUS IN CAMP

mile upon mile, clear to the Arctic Ocean. Somehow that day I was very conscious of that infinite, quiet space.

We threw off our headnets, gloves, and heavy shirts, and stood with the breeze blowing through our hair, gazing all around. We could see, far out over miles of green tundra, blue hills in the distance, on the Arctic Coast no doubt. This was the high point; we had reached the headwaters of the Old Crow. After we had lived with it in all its moods, been down in the depths with it for weeks, it was good to know that the river began in beauty and flowed through miles of clean gravel and airy open space.

We used to go ashore to have lunch, for instance, and you wore a headnet; you'd lift the veil and tear a bit in your mouth and put the veil down quickly. And when you washed dishes, every time you took your hands out of the water, they'd be black with mosquitoes. And they're making that sound, all the time.

After enduring the hardships of the Old Crow trip, Mardy felt she could face anything, and her appreciation for the vast, pristine land of Alaska was growing even deeper. The words filling her diaries were a powerful and emotional reaction to the landscape, so different from Olaus's scientific notes.

The family

OLAUS, MARTIN, AND MARDY
WITH MAMMOTH TUSK

Top of the world

MARDY AT THE
HEADWATERS OF THE
OLD CROW RIVER

We stood there for a long time, just looking. This might be our farthest north, ever. If we could only take a giant step and see the arctic shore; we were so near.

Then our eyes came back to the near tundra, the velvety sphagnum hummocks, the myriad tiny arctic plants gleaming in the moss, in the golden light. The Labrador tea had gone to seed, but its sharp fragrance filled the air. In a tiny birch tree, a white-crowned sparrow, the voice of the arctic summer—"You will remember, you will remember," he sang.

McCormick Ranch

MARDY AND FAMILY VISIT FRIENDS
AT MCCORMICK RANCH, 1929.

In the spring of 1927, Olaus was again in Washington, D.C., preparing for a new assignment. Mardy was due to have their second child, and remained at her parents' home in Twisp, Washington, rather than travel across country. So once again, Olaus was unable to be there for the baby's arrival. On May 21, 1927, daughter Joanne was born. On the first of July, Olaus left the East Coast and headed for a new job in Wyoming's rugged northwest corner, where he would undertake a long-term study of the life history of the North American elk. Mardy and their growing family would meet him there as soon as he had found a place to live.

In mid-July, Mardy bounced along in a Model T Ford on a one-lane dirt road that switchbacked over the southern end of the Teton Range. Olaus was waiting for her arrival in the little town of Jackson Hole. She had no idea that this beautiful valley would

Olaus

OLAUS ON THE STEPS OF THE
"PUMPKIN HOUSE," 1932

Because Olaus had studied caribou in Alaska, he was the logical one to be sent here to study the elk. And the way he did it was to get into elk country and live with the elk, and every summer for many summers the whole family went with him.

become their home for the rest of their lives. Alaska would always be in their hearts and minds, but here in the valley of Jackson Hole their work would take on a broader meaning and propel them into the forefront of conservation.

By 1930, Olaus had been assured of at least a few more years' work in the area, so the Muries built their own home on the edge of town. On their first day in the new house, when Olaus had moved the final load and walked in the door as darkness fell, he commented to Mardy, "You know, as I drove up just now, this place looked so warm and inviting, like a big, yellow pumpkin all lit up inside." From that day on, the Murie home was known as "the Pumpkin House." On December 16, 1931, during the first winter in their new home, Donald Murie was born.

Mardy's younger half sister Louise married Olaus's younger

Home
_____

THE "PUMPKIN HOUSE"

Teton Wilderness,
1927

August 18—My birthday,
almost our wedding day,
and how many achingly
sweet memories it brings!
Be it recorded: they have
been three wonderful
years, and we are more
lovers than even then,
and the future beckons
and is rosy.

Camp

Whetstone Creek, Jackson Hole, Wyoming, July 26, 1927— Here we are, my lover and I and our increasing family, having come on another adventure. We have come to a paradise.

half brother, Adolph, in 1932. They had become friends over the years of Mardy and Olaus's courtship and marriage, and were both committed to the preservation of wilderness. Adolph was also a brilliant field biologist himself and focused his work in the Alaskan wilds he had first experienced with Olaus.

Olaus's reputation as a field naturalist was growing, and he was also forming his own concepts of conservation and wilderness. One of his friends at this time was Bob Marshall, who had heard tales of Olaus and Mardy when he had visited the Koyukuk country in Alaska, and had later invited them to visit him in Washington, D.C. Years later, Mardy recalled that meeting when writing about her early conservation work:

> One of the most vivid memories of my whole life is walking into the Griggs's living room, where Bob Marshall and Olaus stood together by the fireplace. As Bob took my hand we three looked at one another, and I think we all had the same instant thought: Here is a friendship.
>
> It went from there. There was no period of "getting to know." We knew. There was a dinner dance at the Shoreman

Woman's Work

MARDY WITH OLAUS'S MOTHER, MARIE MURIE, AT WHETSTONE CREEK CAMP, 1929

So many women have said to me, "My goodness, how did you manage raising children in the wilderness, wasn't that awfully hard?" I would say, "Think of all the things I didn't have to do. I didn't have to go to a bridge party, I didn't have to wax the floor, I didn't have to answer the telephone, I didn't have to be on a committee."

Dr. C. Hart Merriam

MARDY, DR. MERRIAM, AND OLAUS
VISIT IN WASHINGTON, D.C.
DR. C. HART MERRIAM WAS ONE
OF THE FIRST ECOLOGISTS, AND WAS
IDOLIZED BY THE MURIES.

that Bob gave for several of his friends. How he loved to dance! There was also, of course, great discussion about the wilderness of Alaska as well as other wilderness and how to protect it. But all the talk was spiced and enlivened by his lively pixie sense of humor, his quick vision and imagination.

In a summer soon after that Bob visited us for a few days at our home in Jackson. Our children were entranced by his tales; he had such quick rapport with them, such quick understanding.

Bob Marshall
with niece Pam on
ship, ca. 1935

*In 1934 Bob Marshall
and some close friends
had been on a several
days' hike in the Great
Smoky Mountains.
Coming back down the
trail on their last day
they stopped to rest, and
got to talking about
where they had been
and what they had
savored, and how long
would it be that way?*

*They decided right
there that one more
organization was
needed in the U.S.—
"an organization of
spirited people who will
fight for the freedom of
the wilderness."*

OTTO GEIST AND OLAUS ABOARD
THE USMS *BROWN BEAR*

Olaus had finished the time-consuming fieldwork portion of his elk research in the early 1930s, giving him time to participate in other studies. Olaus went on a 1935 summer waterfowl census in British Columbia, and Mardy and the children camped with him and explored that part of North America. The next year, he was assigned to conduct a biological survey of the Aleutian Islands aboard the USMS *Brown Bear*. Mardy took the three children and sailed with him as far as Seward, Alaska, then went on to Fairbanks for the summer while Olaus finished his work in the Aleutians.

In 1935, Bob Marshall and other conservation visionaries, including Olaus Murie, formed The Wilderness Society, with Olaus as an officer and director. Mardy assisted as Olaus's secretary and was respected as one of the few people in the group who had a lifetime intertwined with wilderness. It was well known that it was a visit to Alaska's Koyukuk country, where Olaus and Mardy had honeymooned, that had also inspired Marshall to see that landscape preserved.

In the Aleutians

In April 1937, I was directed to join the ongoing Aleutian Islands Expedition (1936-38) under Olaus Johan Murie. What a rich prize and privilege the assignment was. Our chief mission was to make a "wildlife inventory" of those treeless, nearly unpopulated islands that reach for eleven hundred miles westward from the Alaska Peninsula.

—Victor B. Scheffer, from Adventures of a Zoologist

Olaus Murie paints
a Laysan albatross
on the deck of the
USMS *Brown Bear*
off Tanaga Island,
Alaska, August 5, 1937.

Caribou hunt

OLD FRIENDS CLARA AND JESS
RUST AND MRS. O'HARA BY CAR
AND TENT, 1937

Olaus was back in the Aleutian Islands in 1937, and Mardy took the children and stayed with Jess Rust's family in Fairbanks while she worked for their friend Otto Geist. After they had met on the Muries' 1924 honeymoon aboard the river steamer *Teddy H,* Otto had devoted much of his time to studying the Eskimos on Saint Lawrence Island, out in the Bering Sea. He had compiled many volumes of notes detailing his archaeological digs and his eight years of living with an Eskimo family. Mardy was persuaded by

MARDY'S SCRAPBOOK PAGE

Island Between

CHRISTMAS CARD MADE FROM
PHOTOGRAPH OF MARDY AND
FRIEND JEAN BUNNELL, DURING
THEIR BOAT TRIP TO SAINT
LAWRENCE ISLAND, 1937

Otto and by Dr. Charles Bunnell, the president of the University of Alaska, to use her talents to write a book based on this work. The result was *Island Between*, a work of historical fiction about Eskimo life before the arrival of non-Natives in the Arctic.

Bob Marshall died unexpectedly in 1939, at age thirty-nine, on an overnight train from Washington, D.C., to New York, and the fate of The Wilderness Society became uncertain. However, he had left the Society a third of his estate—more than half a million dollars—so the vital conservation work could go on, and Olaus and others assumed new responsibilities without Marshall's leadership. That year also brought the death of Olaus's mother, who had lived with the Muries in Jackson Hole since 1930.

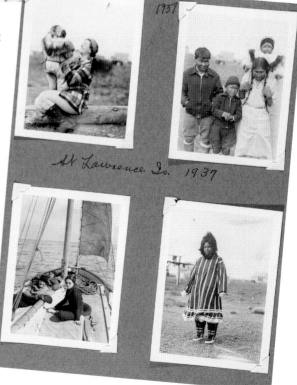

Family, 1930s

▸ Mardy, her
three children,
Louis Gillette, Olaus's
mother and sister
▾ Family life in
Jackson Hole
▾▸ Mardy with group
under elk horn arch,
Jackson, Easter Sunday

Three sisters

MARDY, CENTER, WITH HER TWO HALF SISTERS, CAROL AND LOUISE

By 1940, Olaus's elk studies in Jackson Hole were completed, and Mardy and Olaus made several excursions to observe isolated populations of elk in the western United States. World War II entered the Muries' lives in 1941, when their son Martin served in the 10th Mountain Division in Italy, from 1942 to 1945. And when several of the Aleutian Islands that Olaus had studied in depth were occupied by Japanese forces, he was consulted by the U.S. Army in top-secret meetings about the topography and weather of the islands.

War

MARTIN GOES TO WAR, 1943.

Marie Ranch

If I were to walk across the opening beyond the Homestead, into the forest, across the little swale, and into the forest again, then I should look up at my god of the forest, a white fir that is nearly one-hundred feet tall and a perfect spire. If it were possible to climb to the very top of that fir some day in May, I am sure I would look down on a flow of life we cannot see from the ground.

The log house

The house was built as a summer home for a well-to-do gracious lady from Kansas City, but it was planned by Skipper Mapes and built by the Nelson brothers—Charles, Otto, Neil, and Albert—best log men in the valley in 1937. In 1949 Mrs. W. died and her daughters were willing to sell the house.

Mardy was at home in Jackson with the two younger children during the war years and had taken a job at the Bear Paw Guest Ranch in the summers as the head housekeeper. It was a rewarding time for her, with a great variety of guests, stimulating conversation, and spontaneous music sessions. The Bear Paw was one of the valley's finest dude ranches, and Mardy applied her expedition experience to organizing the ranch chores, hiring a foreman, finding a good cook, and signing up housekeepers. Her daughter, Joanne, worked in the dining room, and young Donald was in charge of setting mouse traps in the log guest cabins.

Being on the Bear Paw Ranch all summer got Mardy interested once more in living out of town, and she asked her friends Buster and Frances Estes, who owned another guest ranch, if they would ever consider selling it to her and Olaus. Their seventy-seven-acre STS Ranch was a collection of sixteen rustic log buildings near

Our dear friend Mildred Capron had departed on her big adventure to South Africa, but one day a cattle truck drove in and backed right up to the front porch. There was all Mildred's antique maple furniture from her apartment in Laramie, for us to use in our new home. Maple furniture fits well in a log house. Joanne's current boyfriend helped unload the truck and remarked, "Now all you have to do is pray an elephant gets Mildred."

75

At home, 1940

❦

THE MURIES IN
THEIR LIVING ROOM AT
THE MURIE RANCH

I felt that the government was not able to furnish Olaus with any kind of a challenge, and the sort of study that he would feel he was accomplishing something for the good of humanity. Came a telephone call from Washington, D.C.—would he consider being director of The Wilderness Society? But he said, No, he was sorry, he couldn't live in the city. So, two, three days later they came again on the phone, and said, "How about taking it half-time, half-pay, and stay in Wyoming?" So that's what we did. And it was just as though our lives blossomed, because we were in contact with people who, whether they were lawyers, doctors, businessmen or whatever, had a very keen interest for wilderness, and being perfectly altruistic about saving wilderness. And Olaus and I both felt we could be free to describe how we felt about wilderness and about everything else and it was very smooth and happy compared to what we had when he was with the government.

This piece of river bottom was my favorite spot years before we ever dreamed of owning it. The Moose neighborhood is just below the main part of the Teton Range. Here are the beaver ponds, the old river channel, the lovely mixed forest. Near the river, tall cottonwoods and river-bottom spruces. Farther back, a mixed forest of spruce, alpine fir, Douglas fir, aspen, and lodgepole pine. This is what we walk through on our way to the ponds.

We cannot think of this little piece of Snake River forest apart from the beaver ponds and little sloughs within it—the whole area is a total ecosystem, a living lesson in ecology. And most important of all we cannot think of it or travel in it without knowing the vibrant part of it—the living creatures.

Winter on the ranch

OLAUS ON HIS WAY TO
THE BEAVER PONDS

Olaus and Mildred and I used to talk about a film, to be called "77 Acres." She got a good deal of it into her Wyoming film— but the possibilities are endless in the river-bottom world. We talked about the species of mammals and counted up so many. And the birds, dear me—

Moose, Wyoming, in a beautiful, remote setting along the Snake River, with a full view of the spectacular Teton Mountains. The STS was named for its cattle brand, which was a phonetic abbreviation of its owners' last name. The Estes family unexpectedly decided to sell and move to Arizona, and in 1945 Olaus and Mardy, along with Adolph and Louise Murie, bought the STS Ranch.

Christmas

CHRISTMAS CANDLES IN PAPER BAGS
LINE THE SNOWY PATH TO THE MURIES' FRONT DOOR.

Our tree this year came from the dump ground. We so dislike
cutting a living tree just for those few days. And you should see it!
We all agree it's the best one yet!
        —Olaus Murie, from a letter to the Murie children

The Wilderness Society

According to Aldo Leopold, a thing is right when it tends to preserve the integrity, stability, and beauty of the biotic community. It is wrong when it tends otherwise. This is a strong rule, and he knew it would take a long time to have it either understood or adopted; but he had these ideas, he was articulate, and, as Mr. Nash says, "... was willing to start, to be the prophet of the new order."

At the same time that Mardy and Olaus moved to the STS, Olaus retired from his job with the U.S. Biological Survey to become director of The Wilderness Society. He disagreed with many of the outdated policies of the U.S. Biological Survey, and had finally given up trying to bring change to that bureaucracy. Their children were grown, and the Muries hoped to focus their energy on conservation and wilderness preservation. With Mardy's help, Olaus completed his books, *The Elk of North America* and *A Field Guide to Animal Tracks.*

In 1949, Olaus was awarded a Fulbright grant to go to New Zealand to study their introduced elk herds; the animals were a gift from President Teddy Roosevelt in 1905. Mardy was secretary for the seven-month expedition, living in Invercargill while Olaus and

THE WILDERNESS SOCIETY
HELD ITS ANNUAL MEETING
IN VARIOUS INSPIRING
PLACES, INCLUDING THE
MURIE RANCH. ELIZABETH
OLSON, WIFE OF SIGURD
OLSON, AND MARDY AT
THE TWS MEETING, 1949.

We took time to swim in the little channel of the river every afternoon, and one day a lovely new friend, Elise Untermeyer, joined us for a swim and for dinner, and brought with her Irwin Edman, a famous Columbia University philosopher. We trekked over the trail and across the footbridges and we swam; we had dinner in the big square kitchen of the Homestead; we came over to the big house and sat by the fire. And Irwin looked around and said, "Isn't this nice?" And he talked of many things and kept us all entranced. And he wrote in our new guest book:

> *"There is no help for it, the Furies*
> *Have given me no rhyme for Muries,*
> *They cannot keep me, though, from making clear,*
> *How nice it has been to be here."*
>
> *—Irwin Edman, August 31, 1949*

New Zealand

OLAUS'S FIELD CAMP

When Theodore Roosevelt was president in 1905 he thought it would be nice to give the people of New Zealand some elk. And in 1905 they shipped eighteen elk from Jackson Hole. They got clear down to the South Island of New Zealand and dumped them in the water and let them swim ashore. And then years later somebody began to wonder what had happened to them, of course. So they wanted to know who was the elk expert in the U.S., and naturally it was my husband.

It turned out to be a big expedition, and they were in the bush for ten weeks. Our son Donald, who was just seventeen, went as his father's official photographer.

In the field

OLAUS ASKING THE FOX FOR THE CORRECT CAMERA SETTING

Spode china

SPODE CHINA BOUGHT IN NEW ZEALAND AND SHIPPED TO MOOSE

When we got back to Wellington, Olaus was busy in the museum. I had my own plans. Every morning Donald would say, "Are we going to any more china shops today?" Every morning my answer was, "Yes." And we finally did find, we thought, a pattern of Spode china that would look all right against a log wall in Wyoming.

their son Donald, the expedition's photographer, were in the field. During her stay, she visited proposed parks and attended the Seventh Pacific Science Conference.

Mardy & Olaus

THE MURIES AT THEIR RANCH,
MOOSE, 1953

The early 1950s saw Mardy and Olaus actively involved with the growth and development of The Wilderness Society. But in 1954, Olaus was diagnosed with miliary tuberculosis, the same disease that had taken the life of his brother Martin in 1922.

Ironically, the treatment for that disease involved the use of a wax-dissolving substance that allowed antibiotics to penetrate the protective coating of the deadly tuberculosis bacteria, and that unique substance came from an African bird intolerant of civilization; Olaus's cure was found only in wilderness. He spent fifteen months undergoing treatment at the National Jewish Hospital in Denver, Colorado, while Mardy took an apartment a few blocks away and worked as a secretary for the Izaak Walton League.

When they were finally able to return to Moose, with Olaus healthy again, they hosted the 1954 meeting of The Wilderness Society in their home. Alaska was taking shape as the battleground

Ernest Thompson Seton

One day in Washington, D.C., Olaus was introduced to Ernest Thompson Seton, the famous author. And Olaus said, "Oh, my, I know all your books. My friends and I grew up with them. We just lived Two Little Savages along the Red River in Minnesota. We did everything you wrote about in there, and we built a tipi but we could never make the smoke go up right." And Seton said, "I never could, either."

for conservation, so by the next meeting of The Wilderness Society in Rainy Lake, Minnesota, plans were made for Olaus and Mardy to return to the Arctic. Two National Park Service members, George L. Collins and Lowell Sumner, had proposed setting aside the remote northeastern section of the Brooks Range in arctic Alaska as wilderness, for scientific study and recreation. Olaus Murie had flown over the area in 1951 with pioneer conservationist Sigurd Olson, and was anxious to head an expedition to survey the region on foot.

While Olaus lined up graduate students to assist him, Mardy did the planning, organizing, and purchasing for the summer. In June of 1956, she and Olaus flew into the remote Sheenjek River Valley in northeastern Alaska. With them were three young biologists: Bob Krear, George Schaller, and Brina Kessel.

Mardy and Olaus considered this expedition to be the best time of their lives. Olaus had chosen the upper Sheenjek River Valley for its unique geological and biological features, but it was the more subtle and personal aspects of their summer that made the trip so memorable: serenity, stark beauty, companionship, and discovery. Lobo Lake, at the foot of Table Mountain, became not only their home for the summer, but a symbol of their wilderness ideals.

For the young scientists with them, the Muries were lifelong role models. All three were close to Olaus and Mardy from that summer on, and credited the Muries with providing examples of how to live and work. George Schaller summed up their influence in the introduction of his 1956 report:

> Dr. Olaus Murie, intimately acquainted with the North Country, taught me in his quiet way to observe and appreciate many of the aspects of the wilderness which I had formerly overlooked. Mrs. Olaus Murie, or Mardy as she is known to everyone, with her charm and efficiency was largely responsible for the planning of the expedition, and it was

OLAUS AND MARDY BELIEVED IN TAKING GOVERNMENT POLICY MAKERS OUT INTO THE FIELD.

Last Lake

THE MURIE CAMP IN THE
SHEENJEK VALLEY—OLAUS,
GEORGE SCHALLER,
BOB KREAR, AND MARDY

*As director of The Wilderness
Society, Olaus took two trips
into the Brooks Range, on the
Sheenjek River, in the hopes
that that northeast corner of
Alaska would be made an arctic
wildlife refuge. I think Olaus
felt more deeply about this area
and this idea than any project
we had been involved in.*

Camp life

MEALS AND HAIRCUTS

*Every day in the Sheenjek
started with breakfast and then
we had a big carton of things
like crackers and cheese and
dried apricots, and everybody
made up their own lunch and
all disappeared in different
directions—Bob to find more
wildlife to film, George to look
at everything, Brina to find
birds. And Olaus and I usually
went off together.*

through her efforts that we accomplished everything that we
set out to do. Mardy also astonished and delighted me every
day with the ease and proficiency with which she turned out
delicious meals from humble beginnings. Mardy was, however,
not stuck in the kitchen, but hiked with Olaus far and wide,

bringing back at the end of the day the blossom of a flower or the description of a calling loon, observations which not only enriched our notes but also our minds.

Olaus and Mardy were back on the ranch in Moose, in the summer of 1957, when Mardy noticed a discolored spot on Olaus's back. Sheenjek biologist Bob Krear was visiting the Muries and drove them to Denver, where Olaus was diagnosed with melanoma. He had surgery, and bounced back to continue lecturing and attending meetings of The Wilderness Society.

The Sheenjek

THE MURIE CAMPSITE AT
LAST LAKE

Portraits by William O. Douglas

Just by example, Mardy and Olaus taught us all. They didn't even have to express it. It was just how they felt and what they did that made all the difference. I think Mardy and Olaus, and earlier Brina, had really a very critical influence on what I ended up doing. The Sheenjek was symbolic of everything I did afterwards. Because it had good science, it had exploration of an unknown area, and it had conservation. And those three together really shaped what I have done all these years.

We had a very comfortable camp. Bob is a great builder. He had tables and everything else constructed out of dead spruce limbs. Everything had a use. And he was our barber. A good zoologist has to be a good barber.

As a result of the 1956 trip to the Sheenjek, Mardy and Olaus and a lot of people fought very hard to get the Arctic National Wildlife Refuge established. We fight for the Refuge and for the last great wilderness in the United States. I've traveled in many parts of the world, in the most remote wildernesses, and I don't think people in the United States realize what treasure they have, because there is very little remote wilderness left in the world. It is very hard to find a place that is virtually untouched, so the Refuge is really a treasure not just for the United States but for the world.

—George Schaller, on Mardy and Olaus
and the 1956 Murie Sheenjek Expedition

In 1958 Mardy and Olaus traveled to Norway to visit Olaus's relatives, then to Finland for the International Ornithological Conference in Helsinki. They also spent two weeks in England visiting Mardy's relatives. They sailed both ways between New York and London and, reminiscent of the old days in Alaska, danced and partied each night on the ship. Back in Moose that winter, they celebrated Alaska's vote for statehood on January 3, 1959, and wondered what implications the change in federal government would have for Alaska's wilderness. Part of the answer to that was the creation, by executive order in 1960, of the Arctic National Wildlife Range by Secretary of the Interior Fred Seaton. Mardy remembered weeping for joy with Olaus when they received a telegram with the news.

Mardy and Olaus returned to the Arctic in the summer of 1961. He wanted above all else to spend a bit more time in the

Cotton grass

SHEENJEK VALLEY, 1956

Sheenjek River

The environment is not tailored to man; it is itself, for itself. All its creatures fit in. They know how from ages past. Man fits in or fights it. Fitting in, living in it, carries challenge, exhilaration, peace.

northern wilderness, so they were flown out to their beloved Lobo Lake in the Sheenjek Valley. They set up camp, hiked to nearby sites, and visited with friends who flew in to see Olaus. Still the director of The Wilderness Society, he gained much satisfaction in knowing his efforts had helped preserve the grandeur all around him. After three weeks of peaceful isolation, Olaus and Mardy returned to Moose, Wyoming, for the winter.

The summer of 1962, while driving home from Olaus's fiftieth reunion at Pacific University in Oregon, Mardy had noticed discoloration in the whites of Olaus's eyes—a new sign of his illness. He soon had to return to Denver for more cancer surgery and an eight-week hospital stay. He seemed to rebound, and they spent a winter in Arizona, then returned to Moose while Olaus began to give talks and take field trips again. Much of his time was spent in the effort with writer Howard Clinton Zahniser, who was the executive secretary of the Wilderness Society and chief lobbyist for the Wilderness Act. (The act wouldn't be enacted until September 1964, just a few months after Zahniser's death.)

In the summer of 1963, Mardy and Olaus returned to Alaska once more, and attended The Wilderness Society meeting held at

❧

We have read 438 pages overflowing with love for Alaska, and we hurry to tell our readers throughout the state and elsewhere of this new book, Two in the Far North *by Margaret E. Murie, Alfred A. Knopf, New York, 1962, $5.95.*

The lilting, feminine phrases of Mrs. Murie (wife of the distinguished biologist Olaus J. Murie whose wilderness drawings illustrate the book) embraces the peoples and ways native to Alaska, the rough-refined life of the Interior half a century ago. Varied personalities come to life in these pages, for Mrs. Murie is interested in people, but through them all shines a constantly sharpening love for the "Great Land" itself, for the vastness and singing wildness of tundra and mountain and river.

—From review of *Two in the Far North* in the *Daily Alaska Empire,* Sunday, December 16, 1962

OLAUS AND MARDY AT HOME ON THE RANCH

FOUR GENERATIONS—JOANNE MURIE MILLER AND HER SON BENJAMIN, MARDY AND HER MOTHER, MINNIE GILLETTE, ON THE FRONT PORCH, 1957

Olaus received the Audubon Medal in November 1959. I think he felt happy about it, but these things didn't impress him so much as the day-by-day working for the preservation of wilderness. And that is where he really put his energy. Then, if these recognitions came along, you'd take them with as much good grace as you could, but the real work still has to go on behind the scenes.

Camp Denali, in what was then Mount McKinley National Park. Their old Alaskan friend Otto Geist had died earlier that year, but Adolph Murie was there studying wolves for the National Park Service. He and Louise were reunited with Olaus and Mardy in the mountains where their lives together had started. Mardy was also celebrating the publication of her book, *Two in the Far North,* all about her life in Alaska.

Olaus began to feel weak, so Mardy took him home to Moose. On August 19, their thirty-ninth anniversary, he was admitted to the hospital in Jackson, and he died there on October 21, 1963. Olaus Murie was seventy-four years old. He was born before the first airplane flight and died after the first manned space flight, but in this time of technological leaps, Olaus's mark was left on solid ground. The direction he gave to the conservation movement set in motion a concerted effort to save large pieces of land, wild and intact. To him, the earth was a living organism to be preserved and cared for, not dominated. This is the legacy he left Mardy.

Mardy's favorite photo

OLAUS DANCING WITH THE ESKIMOS ON NUNIVAK ISLAND, ALASKA, AUGUST 1936

A Voice for the Wilderness

HER OWN PASSION FOR THE LAND

October 22, 1963, to the Twenty-first Century

~

The death of Olaus ended a thirty-nine-year fairy-tale adventure for Mardy. Closing up her cabin in Moose, she went to Seattle for the winter to live in an apartment near her mother. Her children had suggested she work outside of the conservation movement to ease the pain of the constant reminders of Olaus, but Mardy found that her

Matriarch

MARDY AT AGE NINETY-ONE, ON A RAFT TRIP DOWN THE SNAKE RIVER

Mardy by the Lake

I remember that after Olaus passed away our son Donald said to me, "Mommy, maybe you ought to think of something entirely different to keep yourself busy with, and that's satisfying to you." I thought about that for a while, and then I realized that wasn't going to alter things at all, because my feeling for natural country, for the trees and the mountains, the peaks, the wilderness areas that are in danger and needed all the help they could have, that I couldn't just walk away from that. It would never leave me, and it hasn't left me.

I could repeat what Olaus used to say: it was really better to be in the thick of the fight than standing in the corner with your face to the wall. So I'd hate to think that all I can do is moan and cry and make a fuss. You have to somehow do more than that. You have to try to influence more people, that's one thing.

Wilderness Bill

LYNDON B. JOHNSON SIGNS THE
WILDERNESS ACT IN 1964 AND
PRESENTS PENS TO MARDY AND
ALICE ZAHNISER.

*I remember the beginnings of
that one—the eight-year-long
effort to pass a wilderness bill—
the council of The Wilderness
Society sitting on the shores of
Rainy Lake in the Minnesota
canoe country, facing the fact
that administrative regulations
were not enough to really
protect wilderness, that we
would be confronted with
endless controversy, as one
area after another would be
threatened, that we needed a
law to apply to all wilderness—
forest, parks, refuges.*

roots in the movement were deep. She went to work part-time for the Sierra Club and The Wilderness Society. She first began to visit schools in the Seattle area to tell her stories to children, then to speak on behalf of Alaska's wild lands and to testify at wilderness hearings in the Pacific Northwest.

By the next spring, she was able to return to her home in Moose for the summer, to face the empty house and quiet meadows that Olaus loved so much. Her mother, Minnie Gillette, came with her, and her children and grandchildren arrived for extended visits. Mardy found that the peace and solitude of the ranch and the ever-present reminders of Olaus gave her the motivation to go on. She resolved to try to finish what they had started.

That autumn of 1964, the diligence of Olaus Murie and Howard Zahniser finally paid off, when the Wilderness Act was passed by Congress, and President Lyndon Johnson prepared to sign it. Both Olaus and Howard were gone, but their widows, Mardy Murie and Alice Zahniser, were invited to the White House. On September 2, Mardy flew out of Jackson on a day's notice and was in the Rose Garden the next morning when the bill was signed. She was given one of the pens LBJ used for the signing, and met with Morris Udall, who would later figure prominently in the Alaska Lands Act. She returned to Moose reinvigorated and ready to plunge back into conservation.

*Howard Zahniser, executive
secretary of The Wilderness
Society, wrote the first version
of the Wilderness Bill in 1956,
in consultation with all our
conservation colleagues. The
Act was signed in 1964. It had
been a long process, but many
of us felt that the long struggle
bore much fruit, for the process
of hearings was an education
of the public, during which
thousands of individuals began
to believe that they were
important, that they could
take part and be effective in
achieving the kind of world
they wanted to live in.*

Mr. Chairman, my name is Margaret E. Murie. I am a staff consultant with The Wilderness Society, a conservation organization of about thirty-five thousand people. Mr. Chairman, we feel that these wild, ocean-washed offshore islands being discussed here today are a unique part of the natural environment of the state of Washington. They are important as seabird nesting sites and as the home of seals and sea lions; they are important to scientific research for the future in ways we cannot even conjecture about in our time; they are important in simply being a bit of untouched wild America.

—on Washington Islands
   Wilderness, March 28, 1967

Mardy had a wonderful friend named Elise Untermeyer, a "woman of means," as Mardy called her, who thought the best thing for Mardy at this point in her life was a big trip to Africa. She invited Mardy on an extended journey, requiring only that Mardy pay for Elise's "one drink before dinner" each evening. They drove around Africa for five weeks, visiting Tanzania, Kenya, and Uganda, and went to all the preserves and national parks. The Murie name opened many doors with biologists and conservationists who were trying to preserve Africa's wildlife habitat. From Nairobi they went to Cairo and journeyed up the Nile to the old Aswan Dam. By fall they were in New York, and Mardy went home to Wyoming.

Back in Moose, Mardy settled in and finished work on a book she and Olaus had begun writing called *Wapiti Wilderness,* about their early years in Jackson Hole. It was published in 1966 and contained their alternating essays of life and work in this frontier valley. In one of her chapters, Mardy wrote:

> The snow, the storms, the wood sawing and hauling and chopping, the skiing or snowshoeing a mile for mail or messages; all this we enjoyed, and gladly paid that price for the ineffable peace and beauty of this place which soon became deeply home.

One of Mardy's lifelong traits was an ability to make wonderful and long-lasting friendships, and after Olaus died there was a steady stream of old friends arriving to visit her and stay a few days on the ranch. One of Mardy's great companions at the time was a woman named Mildred Capon. Mildred had retired from her fourteen years as a registrar for the Episcopal Church along the Yangtze River in China, and was a talented photographer and filmmaker. In the spring of 1967, Mildred decided to make a lecture film on Alaska, and she persuaded Mardy to be her guide. Mildred had a Ford van set up as a camper, and in May the two women left Moose for the North. Mardy was now sixty-five years old. By the time they returned to Wyoming they had put ten thousand miles on Mildred's van, plus they had flown and sailed many thousands more miles. It was a chance for Mardy to get back in touch with the people of Alaska after a four-year absence during a time when

Angus Cameron, who was senior editor of Alfred Knopf Publishers, wrote me and said, "Write me two or three chapters, just about anything you feel like writing." Okay, so I did that, and he wrote back, "That's fine, now write two or three more." I did that, so came the letter, "Don't send me any more, just finish the book, and I'm enclosing a check for advance on royalties."

Two in the Far North was published and Angus wrote and said, "Now write me one on Wyoming." And I said, "I don't know enough about Wyoming." He said, "Well, write about the Wyoming you do know." Well, Olaus at that time loved to write, and so he said, "Let's do this, a book, together. Alternate chapters." And that's what Wapiti Wilderness is.

And now for the book by the Muries, Wapiti Wilderness— pure gold, every word of it, every sketch. "Mardy" and her husband Olaus, happy mortals, never lost a jot of their sense of wonder, from the cradle up. They are steeped in it, and Olaus has died in it. I find it hard to turn to the task of reviewing when flooded with the associations my own wife and I have had with the Muries in the shadow of the Grand Tetons, and in the lake and alpine fastnesses of remotest New Zealand.

This is by no means a posthumous book. It was composed during many years by the joint authors, and molded into final form by Mrs. Murie after she alone remained. Each chapter is headed by the initials of the member of the pair who wrote it. Yet the work is a harmonious unity, flowing without jolt or dislocation.

—*Review of* Wapiti Wilderness, *by Dr. Murphy, curator at the American Museum*

Mildred Capron

MARDY WITH MILDRED CAPRON (LEFT), 1965, WHO TRAVELED WITH MARDY AND LATER LIVED ON THE MURIE RANCH

the state was undergoing many changes. During her trip north on the ferry, she wrote:

We were not long on the ferry out of Prince Rupert before getting the feel of the new Alaska. There was a fascinating mixture of people on board—a pile-driver operator, a young mechanic, a taxi driver. Going through Wrangell Narrows, quiet, under a slow bell, at dusk, everyone watching the close shores.

We talked to so many tourists, and what were they looking for? Size, vastness, magnificence, informality of life, naturalness, mountains, glaciers? Yes, but also glimpses of old Alaska and of the everyday life of people.

In 1968, oil was discovered under Alaska's Prudhoe Bay. This find had huge implications for the state's wilderness, much like the gold rush at the turn of the century. Mardy was back in Seattle again that winter, working as chairperson of the Seattle Mountaineers committee dealing with Alaska, and she devoted herself to monitoring the activity in the north.

The next year, Mardy made a trip to Australia and New Zealand, sightseeing and visiting old friends from the Muries' 1949 expedition. She was never on vacation from her belief in leaving

Australia

MARDY AND FRIENDS,
CANBERRRA, AUSTRALIA

the natural world alone; every chance available, she gave talks on the value of wilderness, visited parks, and passed on the knowledge she had gained over the years. She wrote in her journal her impressions on visiting a dam site on the Gordon River in Tasmania:

> Past beautiful farms and little towns, apple orchards, and hop fields, to a gate house and $1 fee to enter the H&C road to the mountains and the dam site. And then up and up, and into weird geology—white Ordovician, even the good gravel highway white—and then rust and red, and then green and blue of copper ore, and across little streams, and getting up into the western-type brush, and tall ferns and strange flowers. And mountains—short ranges and peaks at all angles, and we climbing closer into them. The Sentinels impressed me so, and The Wedge—dark, brooding purply rock covered with alpine vegetation—the exposed rock a dark, gunmetal surface. The whole region was otherworldly—stark, wild brooding country, with the road—the white, crass stab of man's arrival—piercing it. And then the end of the road and a lookout, where we could

Home

MARDY AT THE RANCH, 1974

We have had, I know, many hundreds of visitors in the past twenty-five years, here on the ranch. Some come with notice, some just come in. I suppose the books we have written have brought in a good many. And there have been college exchange students and visiting scientists from all over the world. Our lives have been so enriched, and it is fun to wonder who is going to drive in next! Once in a while we may feel rather beset and bereft of privacy—then we flee to the swimming hole. But how would we feel if no one ever came? And they come at all hours! And find me in all situations.

I remember one lovely golden autumn day years ago when, in my oldest pair of blue jeans and with an old red bandana on my head, I was up on the roof, pounding all the roofing nails in tight before winter. A car drove in, two men got out, and I heard the voice of our good friend Harold Fabian: "Mardy, come down off that roof. Senator Hunt wants to talk with you."

look down into the narrow gorge of the Gordon R, and see men and pneumatic drills poised on the brink.

Back in the United States, Mardy stayed in Seattle to work for Brock Evans of the Sierra Club. Her mother, Minnie Gillette, had died in Seattle the previous year, at age ninety, so Mardy now lived at the Women's University Club. With each talk or testimony she gave, Mardy became more confident of her ability to be a voice for the land she loved.

Mardy returned to Moose in the spring of 1970. She had decided she was ready to make the ranch in Moose her permanent home once more, and she asked Mildred Capron to join her there. Besides being a good friend, Mildred was also an independent and self-sufficient woman who was perfectly at home in a hardware

Perhaps the real enemy of wilderness is an invalid American dream. Perhaps too late we are learning that a diet of metal and oil will kill us. Perhaps too late we will discover that valid new frontiers exist in the spirit, and in technology, and that no matter where the new frontiers will be, humans cannot do without wilderness. Alaska, the accidental purchase, has left this nation with a storehouse of green wilderness—Vitamin A-1.

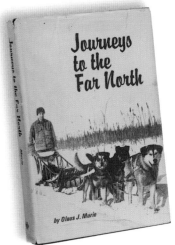

Olaus's book

JOURNEYS TO THE FAR NORTH, 1973, PUBLISHED AFTER OLAUS'S DEATH

Weezy and Ade

LOUISE AND ADOLPH MURIE ON
THE RANCH

store, and she kept the old ranch buildings in shape. Mildred was a
fixture on the ranch until her death ten years later.

Adolph and Louise Murie were still living on the ranch when
Mardy moved back, and until that year they had driven each summer
to Alaska, where Adolph worked for the National Park Service. He
had studied the wolves and grizzlies of Mount McKinley National
Park for years and had published two books on his research. Like
his brother Olaus, he was a dedicated conservationist.

For a National Park Service conference in Alaska in 1975,
Mardy was invited to be the keynote speaker and to remain as a
special consultant for another month and a half. Her task was to fly
all around the state, evaluating areas for inclusion in the proposed
Alaska National Interest Lands Conservation Act (ANILCA). In
many ways, this assignment was a culmination of all of Mardy's
experience in Alaska and her years of working with Olaus and
other pioneers of conservation.

It also promised to be the final chapter in a long fight to

In the field with Celia Hunter and the ANILCA team

Mardy with pilot Ave Thayer

Visiting Dick Proenneke at his remote cabin

Alaska National Interest Lands Conservation Act

Dear Family:

Here is my account of my five weeks in Alaska as a temporary consultant to the National Park Service—one of the most exciting and full periods of my whole life. I have just now finished an eleven page report to Gary Everhardt and hope at least some tiny bit of good may come of my time up north.

On June 23 a meeting was arranged for me with the staff of the Federal-State Land Use Planning Commission; a long discussion of every phase of Alaska planning. I learned a lot. At all times, when I wasn't flying around or running around to meetings, I was in the office of the Task Force, studying environmental impact statements on the various areas, or discussing things with some of the staff.

Flew then westward to Sheenjek lake, and camped there that night, with a cow moose and calf moose feeding and resting on the shore below us. We had a lovely camp-time. I woke at five A.M. and got up and went for a walk up the ridges through all the lovely alpine-arctic growth and moss. After breakfast we all flew southwest to Arctic Village in order to refuel, and then flew north up the east fork of the Chandalar, and through the mountains by a pass, a terrific experience—such gorgeous colors in the stone and the shale and rock of the mountains themselves; emerged onto the green tundra. And soon we were flying along the coast—water next to the shore but ice everywhere else. And on to the Eskimo village of Kaktovik. Refueled, had lunch, flew on east to the Canadian border, turned, topped up the fuel again at Barter, flew west and landed on one of the big lagoons which line the coast. Behind the gravel ridges of the shore the water is almost fresh. It was a marvelous warm sunny day; we lay on the sand and sucked chunks of ice which Dave brought from the outside shore. And then, across on the landward side, we spotted three snowy owls sitting on some humps of tussock.

We flew on west, across the Canning River, out of the Wildlife Range, and immediately there were the signs of MAN—tracks in the tundra, helicopter pads, a gravel road leading off nowhere to where some drilling had been done; piles of oil drums. A relief to turn back into the pristine Range again.

—letter, July 27, 1975

Wilderness Worker

To begin with she was very self-effacing because that had been her role—she'd just stayed in the background and been an encouragement—but when she had to go forth and be in front, she got more and more confident as time went on and became much more assured in speaking to everybody, to congress people or the president or anyone else, about the value of wilderness and the need to protect it.

She simply said yes to the opportunities that came her way to express her feelings, to stand up for wilderness wherever it was threatened, and it grew on her, and it was very becoming.

> *—Alaska environmentalist Celia Hunter on Mardy Murie, from the film* Arctic Dance: The Mardy Murie Story

preserve some of Alaska's untouched wild lands, leaving them much as Mardy and Olaus had experienced them in solitude many years before. As Olaus's secretary for nearly forty years, and an insider in the birth of The Wilderness Society, Mardy had participated in the development of plans and dreams for Alaska's wilderness preservation. She also knew the biology of the Arctic, taught to her by Olaus, so she could back her beliefs with science. This, along with her perspective on Alaska as her homeland and her ability to talk to the people of the state, made her the perfect voice for Alaska's wilderness.

After Alaska achieved statehood in 1959, the fight to divide up its 104-million-acre grant of federal land began. The first of many legislative actions was the Alaska Native Claims Settlement Act of 1971, which among other things ordered the secretary of the interior to identify potential wilderness areas and national parks, referred to as "national interest lands." Some eighty million acres were given temporary protection until 1978 while exact boundaries and designations were determined. Meanwhile, on November 16, 1973, President Richard Nixon had authorized the Alaska pipeline, and its path would take it directly through the Upper Koyukuk region, where Mardy and Olaus had honeymooned fifty years earlier.

For six weeks in the summer of 1975, Mardy flew in a small plane over the proposed parks and monuments with Bob Belous of the National Park Service, ornithologist Dr. Brina Kessel, who had been in the Sheenjek with her and Olaus in 1956, and old friend and Alaska conservationist Celia Hunter. She flew over the Alaska Peninsula and Lake Clark, north to Kotzebue and up the Kobuk

While irresponsible developers—and this does not mean all developers—push to get there first, to get rich first, they fail to realize the greatest resource Alaska has to offer a sick America is clean air, pure water, and wild lands.

And it is not just the developers; without a population that applauded them and purchased their product, they could not continue. The developer may be the hammerhead, but society is the handle and all the power coming down behind it. And as sure as society can smash the hammer down on Alaska wilderness, it can also throw the hammer away . . . and this time around will be the last one.

How much of Alaska for change, for development, for profits, for jobs, for more population? How much for the land itself as it now is, with all the potential gifts of subsistence living, of scientific discoveries, of healthful recreation, of inspiration? On this point, do we have to split and declare war? I plead for a plan under which there will always be room for a healthy economy, for a healthy population, with a great deal of Alaska left alone.

I think my main thought is this: that perhaps man is going

to be overwhelmed by his own cleverness; that he may even destroy himself by this same cleverness. And I firmly believe that one of the very few hopes for man is the preservation of the wilderness we now have left, and the greatest reservoir of that medicine for mankind lies in Alaska.

—Northwest Wilderness
   Conference, Seattle,
   Washington, April 4, 1970

River, on to Cape Krusenstern, over the Sheenjek Valley and up into the high Arctic beyond the Brooks Range.

She flew over the Upper Koyukuk River, and the land passing below stirred her memories of those long winter miles running behind the dogsled on her 1924 honeymoon. She landed in Bettles, where she and Olaus had left the steamer *Teddy H* to take their dog team into the wilderness beyond, and now wrote in her journal:

I got into conversation with the pretty Eskimo woman doing the rooms; turns out she is the daughter of Oscar who was the cabin boy on the *Teddy H* in 1924! When she found out who I was, she said: "My parents have walked up from the old village; they are sitting out there on the grass. You must talk to them."

This was Frank Tobuk, brother of David, who was the pilot of the *Teddy H!* We sat on the grass and talked—he remembered Olaus and Adolph the minute I said my name. We went five miles downriver to Old Bettles, where Olaus and I had spent the month in 1924 in the cabin waiting for freeze-up. I can't talk much about that. The cabin is still standing, but beginning to sink into the ground on one corner. The whole village grown up with willow and cottonwood— no one there anymore. No one went into the cabin with me; I stood in there alone for a few minutes.

Mardy's report and recommendations went into the congressional battle to protect Alaska. She continued to support the passage of this legislation that would preserve Alaska's wild places, and for the next five years she gave interviews, wrote letters, spoke to groups, and testified at hearings. There was a regional hearing on the ANILCA issue held in Denver by the House Interior Subcommittee on June 5, 1977. Mardy Murie was the first in line to speak, and near the end of her statement she said:

I don't know whether the human race is going to survive very much longer; I sometimes wonder whether we deserve to. Who knows what is ahead in the long march of evolution? But saving the last remnants of wild, untouched country seems to me to be the one wise, altruistic, beneficial, and practical action this nation can take for its sanity.

I grew up in Fairbanks while James Wickersham was battling in Congress for a government railroad in Alaska. Wood was the only fuel; hillsides were stripped of birch forests to feed the boilers at all the little placer mines; every household burned ten cords of wood a winter; the waterman brought you two or four buckets of water a day; the nameless hero came in the night to remove the necessary from the privy in the woodshed. Nothing was easy. But everyone counted. Everyone was cared for. They built a beautiful library, and hospitals; there were dress-up parties, homegrown concerts and plays, and always dances. Dance all night, go to the Model Café for breakfast; go home and change and go to work. There were quarrels, but always humor. And we had the "March scandal," too. It was expected— always—at least one!

—Forum on Growth
   in Alaska, June 10, 1975

Dr. Margaret E. Murie

UNIVERSITY OF ALASKA
FAIRBANKS HONORARY
DOCTORATE DEGREE, MAY 1976.
MARDY WITH OLD FRIENDS
MILDRED CAPRON AND UAF
PROFESSOR DR. BRINA KESSEL

*Almost exactly a month in
Alaska, and until now only
the base events recorded in the
little red diary. So I am moved
to record here on this morning
of shifting cloud, rain, and
sunshine, my gratitude for the
overwhelming love and
attention showered upon me.*
  —On the Alaska
    ferry *Malaspina,*
    May 26, 1976

All I have said here could be called emotional,
sentimental, impractical, too idealistic. I am here to plead an
impractical theory, for I firmly believe there are cases where
idealism is in the long run the most practical course and I
believe this is true of Alaska now.

In 1976, Mardy was awarded an honorary Doctor of Humane
Letters from the University of Alaska Fairbanks. She flew there
with her friend Mildred Capron. While she was on the campus, she
was shown the layouts for *Island Between,* her book on Eskimo life
on Saint Lawrence Island, written in 1937 at Otto Geist's suggestion
and set aside for forty years. It was scheduled to be published the
next year, and included all of Olaus's original drawings. Mardy
dedicated it to their old friend Otto Geist.

By the end of that year, time had run out for the temporary
protection of Alaska's wild lands under the 1971 Alaska Native
Claims Settlement Act. A flurry of political deals stalemated, so

*My routine as a writer:
I tried to get the ordinary
housework out of the way
and sit down in front of
the typewriter at about
nine o'clock and stay there
until noon, whether
anything happened or not.
But usually there was
something that I could
be satisfied with. It is a
question of just sitting
in front of the typewriter
and thinking. And the
memories flood in,
they come.*

Island Between *was different. There was so much of it, so much explicit information about
the life of the Eskimos, that I found the only way I could use the material was to make a
narrative. So I simply chose a few characters. I chose a sixteen-year-old Eskimo boy and
called him Toozak. I had all the stories about everything that had happened on the island. So
my book is not fiction. Every incident, everything that happened to anybody, is something
that did happen to somebody on Saint Lawrence Island. It is all material that Otto Geist
collected by living with those Eskimos for eight years.* Island Between *was held up for a
long time because of the Second World War, and then other interruptions came along.*

President Carter

❦

"THANK YOU, MR. CARTER." THE WHITE HOUSE, JULY 21, 1980

Here is the latest saga of your mother's escapades. On July 14 Chuck Clusen, Conservation Director of The Wilderness Society, called me and said that the Alaska Coalition, the "Americans for Alaska" committee et al were planning a doings at The White House on the morning of July 21st; The Wilderness Society was going to give Mr. Carter a "remembrance" in the name of Olaus Murie, and that I was to come and present it to him.

I then made my little speech and handed the book to him and took a seat on a gilt chair on the stage, as I had been instructed. Then Sally Ranney gave a nice little speech and presented a scupture of a grizzly bear. Then next was John Denver, who gave a beautiful talk. The president came up on the stage, shook hands with us who were there, and gave a fine little talk. I am sure he feels strongly about Alaska. Then he turned around and shook hands with all of us, and with the bear!

Well, from there everyone was getting into cabs and going up the Hill, to lobby their Senators!

*And then at six Jim Deane escorted me back for the big party put on by all the groups and by John Denver's Windstar Foundation. John spoke very briefly, then took his guitar and sang us his own Alaska song. It was beautiful, and he is certainly a beguiling young man, who seems to feel very deeply. I had a few words with him the next morning—he had been to Alaska twice at least, and had made a movie, called Alaska—*America's Child.

—letter to family, July 25, 1980

There may be people who feel no need for nature. They are fortunate, perhaps. But for those of us who feel otherwise, who feel something is missing unless we can hike across land disturbed only by our footsteps or see creatures roaming freely, as they have always done, we are sure there should still be wilderness. Species other than man have rights, too. Having furnished all the requisites of our proud materialistic civilization, our neon-lit society, does nature, which is the basis of our existence, have the right to live on? Do we have enough reverence for life to concede to wilderness this right?

John Denver

MARDY AND JOHN DENVER PAUSE DURING THE FILMING OF *ARCTIC DANCE: THE MARDY MURIE STORY.*

Mardy—Thanks to you, we have been able to save the best of the best. May we do more!
—Cecil D. Andrus,
    Secretary of the Interior
    under President Carter,
    from the Murie guest book,
    September 13, 1981

President Jimmy Carter signed a last-minute Executive Order establishing 56 million acres as national monuments and refuges, preserving them until Congress could pass a bill. In July of 1980, there was a party at the White House to thank President Carter for taking this bold step, and Mardy was invited to speak. She handed President Carter a remembrance from The Wilderness Society, in Olaus's name, and made another impassioned statement for the land. At this gathering, she met a young folksinger named John Denver who had also worked for the preservation of Alaska's wilderness. Their lives would intersect again and again in their continuing efforts to keep the Arctic undeveloped.

On December 2, 1980, the ANILCA bill, or the Alaska Lands Act as it was known, was passed. It preserved many of the wild places of Mardy's youth: the banks of a river where a young Olaus stood on his head to impress Mardy and instead surprised an Indian coming downstream in his birchbark canoe, their place

So, what have I said? That we live in a precarious world; that we are threatened by man's ingenuity; that we need a less consumptive lifestyle in order to preserve the beauty and grace of our world; and that our remaining wild places, our wilderness, have to be a most important element in all our thinking and all our doing.

I think if we saved every bit of designated wilderness it wouldn't be enough to satisfy what I think should be the normal longings of a person to know what natural country looks like. And I think just experiencing some fairly untouched country on our planet does something for a person's mind and soul.

You have been called a national treasure and included among the greats of the conservation movement. You have also been described as a connoisseur of swimming holes, a cookie baker extraordinary and, in your own words, a creature of nature.

You grew up in Alaska where you developed your love and knowledge of the outdoor life and became the first woman graduate of its University. You spent your honeymoon in the Arctic studying the caribou migrations with your husband, and for the next 36 years the two of you worked side by side in wildlife research and conservation. Three generations have been moved by your eloquent writings, and today from a log cabin in the shadow of your beloved Grand Tetons you continue to work with young people, instilling them with your reverence for nature.

For your tireless work and lively example as a pioneer in conservation, I am pleased to present you for the degree of Doctor of Humane Letters, Honoris Causa, Margaret E. Murie.

> —James F. English Jr.,
> President, Trinity College
> May 20, 1984

Tea and mentoring

TETON SCIENCE SCHOOL YOUNG TEACHERS GATHER AT MARDY'S.

I've written letters to congressmen, and to forest supervisors, and to national park superintendents. I've testified at hearings, attended a lot of meetings, made a lot of speeches. I'm on the council of The Wilderness Society. I've written some books, traveled in some wilderness. I have also served a lot of tea and made bushels of cookies. But what does that all add up to? There is one other thing, which has simply come my way to do, that has added immeasurable richness to my life. This has to do with working with young people.

There was a time I was trying to make a decision whether to take a job in California or whether to stay. She was listening to it back and forth, and she said, "I'd always go for the adventure." Mardy gave me the sense that you just do it—you don't wait until the time is right.

> —Granddaughter
> Robin Murie

of enchantment—the Sheenjek Valley, and the vast, open tundra without a sign of man.

By 1980, Mardy was known widely as the unofficial "mother of the American conservation movement." The depth and perseverance of her commitment to the land became more evident with each passing year. Others had done much to preserve wilderness, but few approached her lifelong, constant, personal commitment. Although she shunned the spotlight, it managed to find her; in this decade she was awarded the Audubon Medal, the Sierra Club's John Muir Award, and The Wilderness Society's Bob Marshall Award, among many others. She also was given honorary doctorates from Trinity College and the University of Wyoming. She was the subject of countless interviews for radio and TV, including pieces by Charles Kuralt, *National Geographic,* and the *Today* show. Whenever a story was told about wilderness, or when a controversy arose over the value of preservation, Mardy's name came up.

Although she no longer wrote books, she was asked to contribute dozens of introductions to publications on Alaska and the wilderness. She wrote out all of her own speeches, and wrote long and detailed letters to politicians and lobbyists on behalf of

At home

MARDY AT AGE NINETY-FIVE READS
IN HER LIVING ROOM, MOOSE.

*I love to lie awake a little
while at night—listening to
the quietness. Only the faint
sound of the river. There it is,
out there—a piece of natural
world—river and forest and
mountains and sky, and all
the creatures, safely curled up
or wandering about,
according to their various
natures. I lie there and listen,
and feel the nightness of it all.
There is something smooth,
silky, harmonious about the
night, a blessing and a
benison—not simply a gap
between hurried activities.*

conservation of wilderness. One of her more diligent writing tasks at this time was her determination to answer, by hand, all letters written to her. Up to a hundred letters a month arrived at her ranch in Moose—some with queries, some with news, others with just a word of thanks.

The Murie Ranch remained a mecca for conservationists of all levels of commitment, from heads of state to teachers to old Alaskan friends. The ranch was a refuge, and Mardy was always there with an encouraging word, a pot of tea, and a quote to carry out into the world. Mostly, she inspired by example.

She always believed that reaching out to children was one of the keys to conservation. In the late 1960s, she had begun to participate in a local summer program called the Teton Science School, and as it grew into a prestigious year-round environmental education center, Mardy continued to speak to new generations of children. She entertained them with vivid accounts of her own youth in the Arctic, and stressed the importance of leaving wilderness alone for others to experience.

Mardy kept the simple lifestyle she had learned in frontier Alaska—a log home, a wood cookstove, and no television—but she also followed the example of the good women of Fairbanks and maintained a regular social schedule. Every afternoon at four o'clock, she served tea, in summer on the front porch and in winter by the fire. Each Wednesday night, friends gathered in her home to do Crostics crossword puzzles, and every Christmas, she held her traditional cookie swap.

The old STS Ranch, now known as the Murie Ranch, had been sold to the National Park Service in 1968 after Olaus died, but the Muries kept a long-term lease. The ranch was completely surrounded by federally protected land when Grand Teton National Park was formed in 1951. Louise Murie left the ranch in 1977, three years after Adolph Murie died, and moved back into the town of Jackson. She later married Dr. Donald MacLeod, Olaus's physician and a longtime friend. Mardy's lease allowed her to live in her log home for the rest of her life.

Through the 1970s, '80s, and '90s, both Mardy and Louise continued to work in conservation issues. As the significance of the Muries' knowledge and vision became more widely evident, the need for a continuation of their work was apparent. In 1997, with

Memories

MARDY'S HOME IS FILLED WITH
MEMENTOS FROM HER LONG AND
ADVENTUROUS LIFE.

Lincoln Blassy was an Eskimo from Saint Lawrence who carved ivory in the winters, and he would send me a few pieces in the mail along with a few pages of the Montgomery Ward catalog with his selections. I would sell his carvings, or buy some myself, then mail in his order with the money.

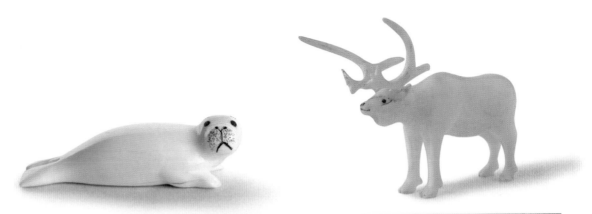

The wonder of the world, the beauty and the power, the shapes of things, their colours, lights, and shades; these I saw. Look ye also while life lasts.

MARDY, WITH HER DAUGHTER
JOANNE MURIE MILLER,
GRANDSON BENJAMIN, AND
GREAT-GRANDSON JOSEPH,
MEETS WITH PRESIDENT AND
MRS. CLINTON AFTER THE
PRESIDENTIAL MEDAL
OF FREEDOM CEREMONY.

the approval and support of Mardy Murie and Louise Murie
MacLeod, an organization named the Murie Center was formed.
Its mission would be to carry on the work and dreams of all the
Muries in speaking for the spiritual value of wilderness. Grand
Teton National Park created a unique partnership with the Murie
Center that allowed the organization to move in and renovate the
seventy-year-old log buildings next to Mardy's home. In 1998,
the entire ranch was designated a National Historic District due to
its importance in the conservation movement. Most important,
the persuasive voices of Mardy, Olaus, Louise, and Adolph would
continue to be heard.

In January of 1998, Mardy boarded a plane to fly out of
Jackson Hole. She had been invited to Washington, D.C., to receive
the Presidential Medal of Freedom from President Clinton.
Fittingly, she left in a winter blizzard that turned this prestigious
journey into another epic journey. At the White House, the President

The President of the United States of America

Awards this

Presidential Medal of Freedom

to

Margaret E. Murie

We owe much to the life's work of Mardy Murie, a pioneer of the environmental movement, who, with her husband, Olaus, helped set the course of American conservation more than 70 years ago. Her passionate support for and compelling testimony on behalf of the Alaska Lands Act helped to ensure the legislation's passage and the protection of some of our most pristine lands. A member of the governing council of The Wilderness Society, she also founded the Teton Science School to teach students of all ages the value of ecology. For her steadfast and inspiring efforts to safeguard America's wilderness for future generations, we honor Mardy Murie.

The White House
Washington, D.C.
January 15, 1998

William J. Clinton

spoke warmly in appreciation of Mardy's personal history and of her commitment to wilderness. The First Lady, Hillary Clinton, introduced the recipients of the award:

> Today, we honor ordinary Americans, but they have accomplished extraordinary things. Each of them would be the first to tell you, as those among them I know have, that they didn't do anything special. But we know better, and we honor them not only for who they are, but also for who they inspire all of us, as Americans, to become.

Mardy Murie died in her home on October 19, 2003. Her life spanned 101 years. She lived that time passionately. For a third of her life she grew up and matured in the North Country, surrounded by the vast emptiness of Alaska and shaped by the magic of the aurora and the midnight sun. A third of her life she journeyed and danced and learned with Olaus, in a time when their environmental vision and commitment were crucial. And a third of her life she gave back to the wild land, the memories, and the enchanted places that had shaped her extraordinary spirit.

Medal

THE PRESIDENTIAL MEDAL
OF FREEDOM AND ITS CITATION
AS IT WAS READ DURING
THE CEREMONY

Murie Center

NATURALIST AND WRITER TERRY
TEMPEST WILLIAMS PROMPTS A
MOMENT OF LAUGHTER DURING
THE DEDICATION OF THE MURIE
CENTER WITH BOARD CHAIRMAN
LEIGH STOWELL, MARDY MURIE,
GRAND TETON NATIONAL PARK
SUPERINTENDENT JACK NECKELS,
KATE STEVENSON OF THE NPS,
AND DIRECTOR OF THE NATIONAL
PARK SERVICE ROBERT STANTON.

A MURIE CENTER CONVERSATION

On Mardy's fireplace mantel sits a small wooden plaque, hand
lettered by Olaus, from a gravestone in Cumberland, England. She
looks at it every day. It says, "The wonder of the world, the beauty
and the power, the shapes of things, their colours, lights, and
shades; these I saw. Look ye also while life lasts."

SOURCES

Arctic Dance: The Mardy Murie Story (film). Produced by Craighead Environmental Research Institute. Moose, Wyo. 2001.

Murie, Adolph. *A Naturalist in Alaska.* New York: Devin-Adair Company, 1961.

——. *The Wolves of Mt. McKinley.* Seattle: University of Washington Press, 1985.

Murie, Margaret E. *The Alaskan Bird Sketches of Olaus Murie.* Portland, Ore.: Alaska Northwest Books, 1979.

——. *Island Between.* Fairbanks: University of Alaska Press, 1977.

——. *Two in the Far North.* Portland, Ore.: Alaska Northwest Books, 1993.

Murie, Olaus J. *The Elk of North America.* Jackson, Wyo.: Teton Bookshop, 1979.

——. *A Field Guide to Animal Tracks.* Boston: Houghton-Mifflin, 1974.

——. *Journeys to the Far North.* Palo Alto, Calif.: American West Publishing Company, 1973.

Murie, Olaus J., and Margaret E. *Wapiti Wilderness.* Boulder: Colorado Associated University Press, 1988.

CHARLES CRAIGHEAD was born in Jackson, Wyoming, and grew up in diverse wild places around the country. He has been a photographer, cinematographer, and writer since the mid-1960s. His camera work has appeared in numerous documentary films and PBS programs, including *Wild Colorado, America's Wild Horses, Grand Teton Wilderness,* and *Yellowstone in Winter.* He has authored the books *Images of Nature—The Photographs of Thomas D. Mangelsen, The Eagle and the River, The Grand Canyon—An Artist's View, Never a Bad Word or a Twisted Rope: Glenn Exum,* and *Who Ate the Back Yard?* He lives in Moose, Wyoming, where he writes and is Media Director for the Craighead Environmental Research Institute. He teamed up with Jackson Hole neighbor Bonnie Kreps to create the acclaimed film biography of Margaret E. Murie, *Arctic Dance: The Mardy Murie Story.* They coproduced the film, which he wrote and she directed.

Award-winning filmmaker and writer BONNIE KREPS was born in Copenhagen, Denmark, and has lived in the United States and Canada since she was a teenager. Her films, most of which have been produced with the National Film Board of Canada, include *No Life for a Woman* and *This Borrowed Land,* and have been screened on CTV, CBC, PBS, and many other television networks in the United States and Canada. Her numerous articles include "Copenhagen at Christmas" for *National Geographic Traveler,* and her books include *Subversive Thoughts, Authentic Passions* and *Loving Without Losing Your Self.* Her films have been shown internationally in museums and festivals.

**Now read Mardy Murie's own words in
her award-winning book, TWO IN THE FAR NORTH.**

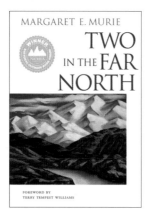

TWO IN THE FAR NORTH
Margaret E. Murie
Illustrations by Olaus J. Murie
Foreword by Terry Tempest Williams

Available in trade paperback with a foreword by Terry Tempest
Williams and expanded text, here is Mardy's classic book, originally
published in 1962. Used as the inspiration and basis for the TV
documentary film *Arctic Dance*, *Two in the Far North* gives the
reader a personal and detailed look into Mardy Murie's life from
her early childhood years to her marriage to Olaus and their lifelong work in studying and saving the wilderness.

Winner of the
National Outdoor Book Award

370 pages, 6" x 9"
10-D ISBN 0-88240-489-X
13-D ISBN 978-0-88240-489-9
Softbound $15.95 USA
CN$21.50

If you enjoyed ARCTIC DANCE, you'll also enjoy . . .

ONE MAN'S WILDERNESS
An Alaskan Odyssey
by Sam Keith

From the journals and
photographs of
Richard Proenneke.
A National Outdoor Book
Award (NOBA) winner.
Over 150,000 copies sold!
10-D ISBN 0-88240-513-6
13-D ISBN 978-0-88240-513-1
Softbound $14.95
CN$24.95

TWO IN A RED CANOE
Our Journey Down the Yukon
by Megan Baldino and
Matt Hage

Follow a couple's summer-
long voyage down the world-
famous Yukon River, from
its headwaters at Canada's
Lake Laberge, along 2,000
westward-trending miles,
to the Bering Sea Coast
of Alaska.
10-D ISBN 1-55868-862-5
13-D ISBN 978-1-55868-862-9
Softbound $18.95
CN$19.95

ARCTIC DANCE
The Mardy Murie Story
by Charles Craighead
and Bonnie Kreps

Own the director's cut of
the critically acclaimed
documentary film as seen
on PBS-TV. Narrated by
Harrison Ford, this provides
an intimate portrait of a
well-loved national figure.
Order directly from
Bob Swerer Productions,
800 737-0239
DVD or VHS $21.95
plus S & H

All books available at bookstores and online booksellers in North America.